Surviving Success

Managing the Challenges of Growth

Jeffrey A. Hansen

The Oasis Press® / PSI Research
Grants Pass, Oregon

Published by The Oasis Press®
© 1998 by Jeffrey A. Hansen

This publication is designed to provide accurate and authoritative information
in regard to the subject matter covered. It is sold with the understanding that
the publisher is not engaged in rendering legal, accounting, or other professional service. If legal advice or other expert assistance is required, the services of a competent professional person should be sought.
> — *from a declaration of principles jointly adopted by a committee of*
> *the American Bar Association and a committee of publishers.*

Editor: Janelle Davidson
Book and Graphics Designer: Constance C. Dickinson
Typographer: Jan Olsson
Cover Designer: Steven Burns
Managing Editor: Constance C. Dickinson

Please direct any comments, questions, or suggestions regarding this book to
The Oasis Press®/PSI Research:

Editorial Department
P.O. Box 3727
Central Point, OR 97502
(541) 479-9464
info@psi-research.com *email*

The Oasis Press® is a Registered Trademark of Publishing Services, Inc.,
an Oregon corporation doing business as PSI Research.

Hansen, Jeffrey A., 1956–
    Surviving success : managing the challenges of growth /
Jeffrey A. Hansen.
        p.   cm. — (PSI successful business library)
    Includes index.
    ISBN 1-55571-446-3
    1. Success in business. 2. High technology industries-
-Management. 3. Small business investment companies—Management.
I. Title.   II. Series.
HF 5386.H2458 1998
650.1—dc21   98-5928

Printed in the United States of America
First edition 10 9 8 7 6 5 4 3 2 1 0

 Printed on recycled paper when available.

For Gabi, Hillary, and Annika

Table of Contents

Foreword

Surviving Success will show you that, as the leader of a growing organization, you must constantly manage the tension between passionately pursuing the most important business priorities and then changing those priorities as needs dictate. This is a difficult and time-consuming responsibility, and it cannot be ignored because failing to either aggressively pursue select priorities or to change them as needed leads to weakness for both the leader and the business.

Surviving Success begins by helping you understand what kind of leader you are. This is critical because, as Mr. Hansen notes, the job of the leader changes over time. The leader must be able to navigate transitions: from decisive visionary in one phase of growth to methodical engineer in another and so forth. What it takes to be a successful leader changes as the situation changes; the leader must therefore champion different priorities at different times. The road map and survival tips will give you the mental framework to make it happen.

As I read this book, I was struck by the insight it provided into my own experience as an entrepreneur leading a company that is now large and diverse. Frank Russell Company is a collection of different businesses, started at different times. It was originally founded by my grandfather in the 1930s as a mutual fund with a local clientele. Since I joined the firm in 1958, we have evolved from a retail mutual fund company to an organization that is a pension fund consultant serving an exclusive niche market of large institutional investors, a trust bank, and a developer of multi-manager funds sold as mutual funds through various distribution partners, large and small, for global distribution.

Today, Frank Russell Company is an investment manager and pension consultant to clients around the world and influences the investment of more than $1 trillion in assets. The business took several decades to grow and, obviously, there were a lot of transitions along the way. Each of these required making critical decisions about business strategy and the type of organization and people we needed in order to meet our goals. While our company of over 1,500 people is considered by many to be quite complex, the conceptual framework for business growth embodied in the *Surviving Success* road map clarifies where we have been and where we need to go.

One of the first innovative breakthroughs that led to our current position transpired much as Mr. Hansen describes in the Concept Development phase. In 1969, I was trying to figure out if there was a way for me to successfully interest pension fund executives in investing in our mutual funds. I got a chance to present my funds concept to the chairman of one the country's leading conglomerates and sold $50 million worth of funds, a sizable piece of business in those days. But I learned something that was much more valuable than that new account: big pension funds didn't want to invest in mutual funds; they wanted somebody to analyze institutional money managers and give them objective rankings and insights so they could make sensible business decisions about how to invest their pension assets. It was an intuitive flash, seeing the broader implications of a single piece of information. As a small, agile organization, we remade ourselves to take advantage of the opportunity. I began calling large pension funds, offering to perform the service of selecting money managers.

The response was so immediate and so positive that I quickly decided to sell the mutual fund sales force I had developed, which was doing quite well with 350 salespeople, and to concentrate on pension consulting. So good intuition helped me to discover the right business to develop at the right time. A few years later, the adoption of the Employee Retirement Income Security Act (ERISA) essentially mandated the kind of investment discipline that we were helping to implement because it made good business sense. It validated the insights we had years earlier. Our pension consulting business has flourished around the world. Its growth has been guided by a series of highly capable leaders who have carried it through many of the phases that this book describes.

In 1980, we realized that the advice we were providing on a custom basis for large pension sponsors could be made available to a larger number of clients through packaging our advice differently. These insights led to our multi-manager funds. This business has been led through its various phases by teams of great people. We have needed all types of leaders at all times. I have long believed that I am an intuitive decision maker and the self-test in *Surviving Success* confirms it. While my intuitive nature led to many successes, it also produced organizational repercussions, in many cases similar to what this book describes, that we have had to address as we have grown.

Viewed through the lens of *Surviving Success,* our continued success comes from our ability to spot attractive opportunities and then structure ourselves to take advantage of them. I believe it's not enough to simply have a good idea. You also have to be able to build on it, sell it, and deliver the promised results. At the same time, you can't rest on your laurels; you can't stop innovating. These changes require different sets of skills. It's important for leaders to be honest about their own strengths and weaknesses so that they can surround themselves with people who bring the needed, complementary skills to the table.

As a success-oriented organization, we have always been interested in the professional development of our people, our most important assets, and we have used a wide range of training. *Surviving Success* does not replace this training but sets the context for it. It provides a guide for the right time to address specific issues. I believe that the overarching message of Jeff Hansen's book, that wisdom, conscious choice, and deliberate action are the most important traits in leaders, is completely true. *Surviving Success* will empower and strengthen everyone to lead with greater success over a wider range of situations. I am grateful for the insights this book provides.

I believe *Surviving Success* will be a valuable tool that we will use as a reference and a guide as we lead our enterprise into the new millennium.

GEORGE F. RUSSELL JR.

Preface

My interest in growing and changing businesses developed at a very personal level. I was born to two entrepreneurs. My father was a geophysicist in oil and uranium exploration, and my mother was an art dealer in the San Francisco area. Both started their own businesses and achieved respectable levels of success.

I had my first view of a start-up business at my father's company where I worked from an early age. My priority was to learn every part of the business, so I started out stacking boxes and sorting rocks. After completing college, I moved on to greater challenges such as accounting and, ultimately, management of one line of the business.

It was then the late 1970s, and oil crises had created what appeared to be an insatiably high demand for new sources of energy. The company's geophysical exploration team of 20 people was innovative, flexible, thoughtful, energetic, and aggressive. It was clear that these traits had a positive impact on the business. The company's reputation was strong, and it was able to get all the business it could handle.

All work done for customers was innovative, thorough, and highly customized. As I learned the business, however, it became clear that not only was the work done for customers innovative and custom, but everything the organization did was innovative and custom. The accounting system was non-standard, personnel policies were unusual, and planning was informal. There were surprises in nearly every aspect of the business.

Technical decisions and business decisions were handled in essentially the same way. Everyone was involved in doing a project for a customer, and everyone was involved in ordering office supplies. Even more telling, Dad's role was the same in both technical decisions and business decisions — he had the final say. He ultimately decided where to sink the next exploratory well and when to order new stationary. Everything in our business was painted with the same brush.

It was clear that the business had reached the limit of what it could accomplish using its existing practices. When a new member was hired to share the workload, more problems were created than solved. The company would grow to a certain point, falter, and grow no further, regardless of the determination of a dedicated team. It seemed unfair for such well intentioned and hard working people to be limited by some unseen barrier.

After several attempts at further growth, it became apparent that, to grow, the company would have to change the way it operated at a fundamental level. Unfortunately, many resisted change. The widespread view was that to change would affect the feel of the company and thus the way people felt about working there. Although the company was considered to be successful by most in the industry, it did not achieve the level of long-term success that many had thought was possible with the energy, insight, and innovation of the people involved. Its initial success could not be sustained as the organization grew and matured. The company was in a weakened state and much more vulnerable to harmful market forces.

My mother's art business depended more on customer service and less on innovation. Yet intelligence, hard work, and good intentions did not lead to persistent success. A decision to expand too early diluted available time, energy, and resources. For her business, too, the management practices that launched the business ultimately inhibited its growth and expansion.

I wondered if the scenarios I had witnessed at a personal level were common in other firms and other industries. In graduate school at Willamette University, I learned the importance of an entrepreneurial leader's personal decision style and that a small firm's business and organizational strategies often mirror the leader's way of making personal decisions. This was an earthshaking bit of news to me. Had my parents been held captive by their characters? Were they being constrained by the very personal qualities that caused them to be successful in the first place?

To answer these questions, I set out to evaluate a large number of successful businesses. It was the early 1980s, and market demand then for high-tech hardware and software allowed many new entrepreneurs to gain a foothold in the marketplace, so there were many companies available to research.

I decided to focus my research on companies selected for funding by venture capitalists. This seemed like a good group of companies to study for three reasons. First, these companies had been carefully evaluated by someone other than me, the venture capital firms, and judged to have good prospects for the future. Second, the leaders of these companies and their growth strategies had been tested by actual market conditions. Third, venture capitalists are relatively quick to replace ineffective leaders, so I had a good chance to see which approaches to leadership are most effective at different stages of growth.

In comparing the various groups of leaders, I found that venture capitalists favor leaders with different styles in different situations. In successful companies, different CEO management styles were highly correlated to different phases of growth. In companies experiencing difficulties, there was no difference in CEO management styles from one phase of growth to the next.

Of course, statistical research did not tell the whole story. For two years I traveled from Seattle to Los Angeles interviewing CEOs of high-tech companies to determine how their management styles related to their business priorities, growth, and success. My conclusion was that different styles of management are indeed more effective at different phases of organizational growth. Problems arise when the business moves from one phase of development to the next but the leader and the organization fail to keep pace with the changes. Therefore, the challenge for the leader is to promote the priorities needed for business success in each phase of development and to have the flexibility to promote different priorities when the situation changes.

Since 1986, I have evaluated over 200 of the most prominent investment firms in the United States, Japan, and Europe as a part of my work with the Frank Russell Company. Two features of investment firms made them excellent for the study of leadership and organizational effectiveness. First, investment firms are essentially pure decision-making organizations. The main purpose of an investment organization is to collect information from a wide variety of sources, process it, and make and implement decisions. In order for them to make money for their clients, they need to collect better information, process it faster, develop better insights in the interpretation of the data, and implement the resulting decisions faster than their competitors. These demands on investment firms make the efficiency of the decision-making structures crucial to their success. Weak decision-structures don't survive.

Second, measuring the results of their decision-making efforts is a relatively objective process. Their success is indicated by numerical investment performance, and this performance can be evaluated against objective benchmarks, stock market indices, and the performance of other firms. Therefore, it is easy to tell who has made good decisions and who has not, regardless of their marketing claims or how rich the people have become.

Objective measurement also makes it possible to compare the relative success of two different organizations that use different types of decision structures. One may be a large, established firm located in one of the world's financial capitals; another may be a small firm located in a town in middle America. Both produce portfolios that will be compared side by side, based solely on the success of their decisions.

For these reasons, investment organizations give a clear indication of which leadership and decision-making approaches are effective in different situations, despite the specialized nature of the business. I discovered that the pattern of growth and development of investment management organizations generally fits the same pattern I'd seen in innovative high-tech organizations. For these reasons, I believe the research behind *Surviving Success* makes it a useful guide for various types of business.

My research on high-tech organizations, which is the basis for the road map in *Surviving Success*, was recognized in 1985 by the National Association of Small Business Investment Companies (NASBIC). It was from this research that I concluded that my parents were indeed ultimately hindered by their personal attributes that had given them their most dramatic successes. Nevertheless, this is not to say that you will not be effective in a certain situation because of some aspect of your personality. It is not about trying to change who you are. Instead, the purpose of this book is to help you expand the range of situations in which you will be effective by giving you a broader perspective on your situation, much as a map can show you something about what lies beyond the next turn.

I hope that this guide will help you achieve personal and business success.

Acknowledgments

I am grateful to many people for their support and encouragement over the years when I conducted research for this book and then toiled with how best to present my thoughts.

Special thanks go to several people who supported the initial research of high-tech companies in the early 1980s. Clay Myers, then Treasurer of the State of Oregon, enlisted the support of some of the nation's leading venture capital firms. Dr. Alan Rowe's work on decision styles enabled me to understand the dynamics of organizational growth more objectively.

Wayne Kingsley representing the National Association of Small Business Investment Companies (NASBIC) was a supporter of the ideas that emerged from the early research. Jerry Wilson, the visionary CEO of Soloflex, shared with me his views on organizational dynamics and encouraged me to delve deeper into the human element of business growth.

I have always believed that my views are best understood by reading a book. One can read ideas that challenge one's established ways of thinking and assess the relevance of the ideas without the fear of being influenced or judged by others. Thus, determining the best way to present the ideas in writing has been a major effort over the last few years.

I am deeply indebted to the many people who have helped me shape the message for this purpose. Julie South and Shirlee Christensen provided unending encouragement and editorial advice. I also thank Paul Warnock, Nick Nesland, Michael Sheldon, Kyle Hansen, Roger South, John Wells, Dori Jones Yang, Masanori Tsuno, Bill Jacques, Arnie Prentice, Dave Jepsen, Ayumi Sasaki, Blake Westley, David Matteson, Dan Sisson, Don Utter, Alan Brownsword, and Heidi Waldrop for patiently working through the various drafts of the work with an insightful and critical eye. If I have failed to attain the goals they have set for this book in terms of clarity and impact, I alone am at fault.

The people at PSI Research/The Oasis Press also have my sincere appreciation for their diligent pursuit of quality: Emmett Ramey for his support for this project; Janelle Davidson for her conscientious edit; Jan Olsson for his typographic wizardry; Steven Burns for his excellent cover; and C. C. Dickinson for her patient, skillful management and her meticulous book design and graphic work.

I would also like to acknowledge and thank my friends and colleagues at the Frank Russell Company who place a high value on understanding the impact of leadership on organizational effectiveness. This perspective has kept me on track over the years.

I also express my deepest thanks to my family and friends who have stood by me over the many years of research and writing.

Very special thanks go to my parents for their rich examples of business leadership and, more importantly, their belief that working hard and working smart is a dynamite combination.

Introduction

If you are going to travel through unfamiliar territory, any kind of information about its different regions, rivers, mountain peaks, cliffs, and gorges will help you get through it more quickly and successfully. Even if you have traveled through the territory before and it is somewhat familiar, a map will help remind you of where the hazards are that can slow progress or cause you to turn back.

Detailed maps exist for some territories. For others, maps do not yet exist, and the best guidance comes in the form of stories from those who have traveled through the territory. Both the map and stories can warn you of the dead-end paths and where the rockiest terrain is.

Surviving Success is a road map of the terrain traveled by the leaders of growing and changing organizations. The examples in this book are based on real businesses. Some are prominent and some small, but the names, places, and specifics of their businesses have been changed to protect the confidentiality of those who have shared their struggles and challenges.

The purpose of this book is to describe the paths different people take through the territory so that others will be able to make better choices about what path is right for them. The book's compilation of experiences, research, analyses, and conclusions is meant to help you avoid some of the hazards that lie ahead.

You will read about:

- Five phases of business development for your new venture.
- The five modes of operation that correspond to the different phases of development.
- Each mode's characteristic organizational structure, cultural priorities, and means of control.
- The management style that is naturally most effective for each mode of operation.
- Key indicators that your business is moving from one phase of development to the next and that it is time to adopt a new mode of operation.
- The classic undesirable legacies of past successes, which reveal that your problem is based in a practice held over from an earlier mode of operation.
- Ten survival tips to improve your ability to lead your organization through a wide range of situations.

This book will help you understand the extent to which your personal management style influences decisions you make, priorities you set, how you structure your organization, and the organizational culture that develops within your organization. You will be better able to make choices about these important variables to foster continued growth and success. You will understand how your relationship to your firm can be kept interesting, challenging, and rewarding. You will have a better sense of alternative paths that can meet your business objectives and be prepared to successfully manage the challenges of growth.

Chapter 1

Success Is Just the Beginning

The Road Ahead

Survival Tips

Success Is Just the Beginning

If you're an entrepreneur or a member of an entrepreneurial team, you probably dream of creating a great company that reaches many people and outlasts you. Yet most startups fail, and very few entrepreneurs are able to lead their companies through the many business stages to corporate sustainability and maturity. The irony is that most businesses fail because their leaders continue promoting the same management priorities that succeeded at an earlier stage.

What they need and what you need is a road map, an early heads-up on the various phases your company needs to pass through on its way to lasting success. No two companies are the same, but there are certain predictable phases of development. If you know about these in advance, you're more likely to stay in control of your company and steer it safely past the various hazards.

Many of the legends in the business world built their enterprises on their visions and passions. Henry Ford, J. P. Morgan, John D. Rockefeller, Bill Gates, and others pushed new frontiers, changed the business landscape, and experienced phenomenal successes. Their visions and their companies affect our lives every day. But the most astonishing feat accomplished by these visionaries was that they built on their initial start-up success to lead their companies on to industry dominance. They realized the dream of growth and success that so often eludes the entrepreneur.

The more common experience, however, is that the creative visionary and his or her company achieve initial success and then both falter as the business grows. The thrill and camaraderie of early success give way to anxiety and panic. The organization fragments, the leader fears losing control, business opportunities are missed, and internal management issues consume ever larger shares of management attention. Poor decisions are made and the business weakens.

What is the cause? Has the leader suddenly become a bad leader? Perhaps. Has the staff become a collection of malcontents? Perhaps. More likely, the fundamental problem is that the situation changed and a new approach to management was needed.

It often happens that the organization and the leader each react differently to success. After a period of success, an organization grows, and as it grows it places new and different demands on the leader. The leader, however, emboldened by success, continues with renewed vigor the same management practices and priorities that were effective in the past. All too often the leader does not see that new practices are needed.

Some practices that are instrumental to survival and success during one phase of development are poorly suited to the next. If a leader persists in using them, future growth and development are hindered. In addition, historically successful practices often become enshrined in the organization's culture to the point where they hinder the company's ability to adapt. In this unfortunate situation, the business does not get the leadership it needs, the leader feels out of step, and business suffers. Consider the example of an entrepreneur who will be called Carl.

Carl's Young Company

Carl loved to create new mechanical tools, and he started a machine tool company in the Midwest centered around his own innovations, primarily one they called the Model 1000. Carl's organization evolved quite naturally at first. Its structure was informal and flexible, and it could readily adapt to Carl's new designs and initiatives. Everyone pitched in to get work done, and the company enjoyed spectacular initial success because customers appreciated the innovative tools Carl created.

But after a period of initial growth, the company stalled. The staff of 25 people seemed to be going in 25 directions. They became profoundly disillusioned. Carl couldn't figure out what was wrong. He made several attempts to resuscitate the firm by reasserting his vision and personal control. This strategy had been successful early on but was of no help now. Carl wanted help fixing his company.

After a review of the business and its products, it was clear that Carl's company simply couldn't keep up with Carl. The challenge of refining, manufacturing, selling, and supporting all the products Carl could create was more than could be handled effectively by the organization Carl had built. The informal structure of the organization, which flowed quite naturally from Carl's style of management, simply could not support a larger operation that could excel in efficient manufacturing.

Carl's problem was that his management style deeply affected the entire organization. His personal behavior as leader influenced how everything was done on a day-to-day basis, even if he was not directly involved. Because he placed high priority on creativity and custom work, the priorities that had launched the business, these were the priorities that his employees observed in their activities, and most things were done in a creative and informal manner.

The demands placed on the organization were changing, however. Business success was being influenced less by the creation of new products and more by the ability to manufacture existing products efficiently. By continuing to be informal and creative, Carl's business suffered. By reasserting his personal vision and control when faced with mounting difficulties, Carl did what was rational; he continued doing what had been successful for him in the past.

Even if Carl had sensed that change was needed, however, his staff would have resisted. Being informal and creative had become a part of the culture of Carl's organization. The staff had become accustomed to this mode of operating and equated it with success, their own identities, and the identity of the company.

The answer for Carl was first to recognize the impact his management style had on the firm and then to understand the limitations that this imposed on his company. Soon, Carl could identify and implement the structures and priorities that were right for his company and the new business opportunities it had. He could then shape the culture to remain flexible and to be supportive of success in different situations.

To try something that has not been proven successful goes against reason. For Carl to discontinue once-successful practices took understanding, wisdom, and courage. Because his natural style of management was, of course, his preferred style, it also involved accepting some personal discomfort in exchange for achieving greater business success.

Fortunately, when entrepreneurial leaders understand the impact of their management style and behavior on their organizations, they can make a conscious choice to alter their management practices. They begin to bring the structure, culture, and priorities into alignment with the requirements of their business opportunities. Ultimately, their flexibility allows them to remain effective over longer periods of time and in a wider range of situations. Leaders who survive one phase of success to be successful in another place a higher value on success than on doing things in their own particular ways.

The Road Ahead

The cold reality is that most of the people who now survive success can do it because they haven't in the past. They have learned the hard way, by making mistakes and learning from them. This learning process requires time, an opportunity for another chance, personal tenacity, introspection, and a tolerance of personal discomfort.

Although the learning process takes time, having a clearer view of the path ahead and seeing your situation from a broader perspective can reduce the time required. If you can see the subtle indicators that change is afoot then anticipate and prepare for the changes before they become imperative, you will stand a better chance of surviving.

Fortunately, new ventures pass through reasonably distinct and predictable phases of development. By understanding these phases you can prepare for each upcoming phase. You then have a better understanding of what will be required in terms of leadership and problem solving.

As indicated by the Phases of Business Development and Modes of Operation chart, a business generally moves from left to right as it grows and develops, although the sequence of phases is not the same for all businesses. The phase is the situation; the mode is how you respond. The phase is the shape of the hole; the mode is the shape of the peg. An organization is most effective when its response is best suited to the situation, when the shape of the peg is aligned to the shape of the hole. The distinction between a phase and mode is:

- A phase is a period of time in the development of the business dominated by certain types of issues, and
- A mode is how the organization operates as it addresses the issues.

Phases of Business Development and Modes of Operation

Phase of Business Development	I. Concept Development	II. Foundation Building	III. Rapid Market Expansion	IV. Market Stabilization	V. Niche Development
Appropriate Mode of Operation	Innovating	Restructuring	Producing	Planning	Adapting

The key to all survival strategies is the same: survival is the result of wisdom, conscious choice, and deliberate action. It is the ability to do the right thing at the right time. It is not the result of any single management style or set of priorities.

The following chapters will detail each of the phases of development, the modes of operation, and the problems encountered when changing from one mode to the next. Also covered will be various management styles for the leader as well as structures and priorities for the organization. A road map diagram will be introduced later to help you understand the choices before you.

Survival Tips

Before you read on, note the ten survival tips given here. As you read the book through, these survival tips will take on deeper meaning.

These ten survival tips are practices that will increase your ability to lead your organization through a wide range of situations.

1. Know yourself. An understanding of your preferences will help you identify what effective practices are likely to develop as a natural result of doing what you like to do, as well as those that will need to be the result of a conscious decision.

2. See your situation objectively. Try to see the true nature of the management situation as opposed to seeing what you would like it to be. Understand the true requirements of the management situation.

3. Allow personal and organizational objectives to diverge. Over time, your organization's objectives will begin to evolve independently from your own. Be ready for those times, both personally and as the leader of the organization.

4. Look for deeper issues in daily problems. Seemingly incidental problems are sometimes indicators of deeper problems in the organization. Be on the lookout for indications that it is time for major change.

5. Use business momentum wisely. Success builds business momentum, and you can use this momentum to carry you through periods of restructuring.

6. Anticipate and plan for the changes that lie ahead. Use the easy times to plan for needed changes. Some successful practices will take time to develop, and you will need time to prepare.

7. Work with and through others to achieve objectives. You will discover that, as you create different modes of operation, some will come naturally and some won't. The intelligent use of others will increase your survival rate dramatically.

8. Sculpt the culture of the organization. An organization's culture is sometimes the most powerful force determining how its members act. Seek not to limit the culture but to enlarge it to support the different practices needed in different situations.

9. Broaden your own range of leadership skills. Learn skills and techniques from others who are naturally well suited to situations you find difficult. Follow their lead and emulate their practices and priorities.

10. Find ways to make natural tendencies pay. Look for ways to have people do what they like to do. They will approach tasks more energetically and passionately.

These disciplines will enable you to break free from the barriers to growth created by preserving once-successful practices in situations that require other approaches.

Chapter 2

Phases of Development and Modes of Operation

Phases of Development and Modes of Operation

As you take your business from startup to a sustainable enterprise, your business, product, and customers will change and go through different phases of development. This chapter explains five general phases of development along with the corresponding mode of operation most effective for each phase.

Each mode has a characteristic organizational structure, set of dominant cultural values, and most effective management style for the leader. The purpose of each mode is to meet the most pressing needs of its respective phase of development. If the needs are met, beneficial legacies can be created. Inevitably each mode produces a certain amount of undesirable baggage that gets handed on to the succeeding phase. These undesirable legacies often create the most intractable problems a growing firm can have. By understanding how all these variables combine and change over time, you can better understand how your organization fits into and responds to its constantly changing business environment.

Phase I – Concept Development

Most people start a new business hoping to develop a breakthrough innovation that will save their potential customers time or money or give them the ability to do something they want to do. Your business opportunity is to do something qualitatively better that will encourage customers to change their spending habits and support your company.

The mission of the firm during this phase is to develop the breakthrough innovation. The most pressing objectives are to refine the vision, to determine how the vision can be realized in a product or service, and to validate its marketability.

Your first customers are likely to be pioneers, people who are enthralled by your innovation, regardless of whether or not its benefits are clearly understood, or who are willing to take a chance with you in order to be the first in their neighborhood to own and benefit from the innovation. While they do you the favor of giving you business, they ask for special treatment in return.

The Innovation Mode

The Innovating organization has the structure of a team of focused generalists. It is small and informal, and everyone can sit around a table and be involved in every decision. Although the leader ultimately makes most decisions, there is an all-for-one and one-for-all atmosphere. Most of the members wear many hats. The upper limit for the number of people that can be meaningfully involved is 10.

The most naturally effective management style for the leader is that of a decisive visionary. The beneficial legacy of this mode is a solid foothold in a market niche.

Phase II – Foundation Building

Once a profitable new product idea has been created and validated in the marketplace, the most important objectives for your business are to:
- Simplify the product and product line,
- Make business processes more rational and formal,
- Build an infrastructure capable of supporting the production of the product and a larger business, and
- Identify the market segments that, if successfully served, will expose your product to the greatest number of attractive market segments.

This is clearly a phase for restricting existing activities and preparing for future modes of growth. During this phase your customers are essentially the same as those you had before. They key difference is that you need to look at them differently in preparation for the future.

The Restructuring Mode

During this mode, roles and responsibility are clarified and formalized, accountabilities assigned, policies developed, and structures established. When you first you encounter this after the Innovation mode, work will need to become more narrowly focused; members can no longer wear as many hats as before. This transition is most easily done when you have from 10 to 25 people in your organization.

The most effective organizational structure is the functionally segmented team. The most naturally effective style of management for the leader is that of the collaborative engineer.

The beneficial legacies of the first experience of the Restructuring mode are an efficient initial business infrastructure and a simplified version of the breakthrough innovation that is suitable for high volume production.

You will need to use the Restructuring mode between the other modes of operation as your business moves through its various phases of development. Although the early growth and development of your business should consist of the Innovating and Restructuring modes in sequence, the remaining sequence of modes can vary, depending on your business conditions and opportunities. There is no single sequence that is right for all organizations.

An opportunity for moving on to the Rapid Market Expansion phase may present itself. Or your business may move quickly or even directly to a Market Stabilization phase or perhaps a Niche Development phase.

Phase III – Rapid Market Expansion

The mission of the company during this phase is to expand market presence as rapidly as possible.

Some firms are fortunate to have the opportunity to experience significant growth based primarily on a single, simplified version of its innovative product or service.

During this phase, your customers are largely pragmatists, people who are highly practical but who will be early adopters if the product clearly delivers the benefits of the basic innovation and if they are confident that the product and your company will become industry leaders. You can offer these customers a relatively simple product at a premium price. Obviously, not all businesses are lucky enough to encounter a large group of such customers.

The Producing Mode

Effective producing organizations are focused and results-oriented. The organization is structured as a platoon of implementors. Decision making is centralized and focused on a relatively simple objective: sell more. Action is valued. The naturally most effective management style for the leader is that of decisive commander. The beneficial legacies of this mode are broad market exposure, high market share, and money in the bank. The signal that this phase is coming to an end is the onset of serious competition. If you have done well, competitors will want a share in this expanding market.

Phase IV – Market Stabilization

With more competitors crowding the field, your business may go through a stabilization phase during which competition is based on price, reliability, and consistency. The most attractive business opportunity is often to serve the large group of customers who are conservative in their buying behavior. These conservative customers desire a low-cost, high-quality product that does not require them to change their lifestyle to use it.

The most important objectives during this phase are to:

- Define the features needed to attract these conservative buyers;
- Develop greater efficiency in the firm's main functional areas, such as manufacturing, sales, or accounting; and
- Reduce the cost of production.

The Planning Mode

Planning organizations are formally structured as a pyramid of functional groups. Work is divided into functional components and assigned to departments to handle that function. The output of these groups come together in a predetermined fashion. Predictable behavior and follow-through by all members are highly valued. Clear accountabilities and responsibilities are important. The naturally most effective management style for the leader is methodical engineer. The main beneficial legacies are powerful functional capabilities and employees who are well trained in the details of the functional activities.

Phase V – Niche Development

Once you have a highly refined product, efficient production capabilities, and staff with high expertise, the most attractive business opportunity may be to develop customized products for niche markets. Customers during this phase may have been interested in your products in the past and may have already been purchasers, but they believe their situations are unusual and require more customized solutions. They can be sophisticated customers and are willing to pay more for additional benefits. Important objectives are to:

- Become familiar enough with the various market segments to initiate the appropriate customization,
- Identify the similarities among various market segments that will enable greater standardization, and
- Watch for opportunities for breakthrough innovation.

The Adapting Mode

In the Adapting mode, the appropriate structure is a federation of market-driven teams. Decision making is decentralized, and work is portioned out to groups specializing in specific segments of the market. Being creative and listening to the customer are highly valued. Vision, cross-functional teamwork, and relationship management are key themes. The most naturally effective management style for the leader is that of collaborative visionary.

The beneficial legacies of this mode are that staff develop the habit of listening to the customers and the company continues pursuing developmental innovation.

The Business Potential Typical of Different Phases

The different classes of buyers you serve in the different phases indicate their business potential. The classes of buyers described here are based on the technology adoption cycle described by Geoffrey Moore in *Crossing the Chasm* and *Inside the Tornado*.[1] The technology adoption cycle refers to the timing of when people tend to accept, or adopt, new technologies or products. In the diagram below, classes on the left adopt early. Those on the right adopt late. The business potential of these classes can be represented by the normal distribution curve as shown on the next page.

---

[1] Geoffrey A. Moore, *Inside the Tornado* (New York: HarperCollins Publishers, Inc., 1995). The model developed by Geoffrey Moore focuses on high-tech businesses and has been modified here to correspond to the phases of business development and modes of operation.

Classes of Buyers

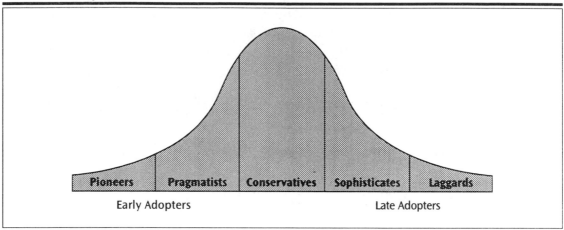

Each of the segments in the bell curve represents a different class of buyer, based on how quickly these buyers will adopt the innovation, the reasons they buy the product, and what qualities they value in it. For new products, and change in general, acceptance moves from left to right.

Pioneers

These are the revolutionaries who want to benefit from the novelty of innovation, to make a break with the past, and to start an entirely new future. Their expectation is that, by being the first to exploit the new capability, they will achieve a dramatic advantage over the status quo. They believe in revolutionary change and are genuinely interested in new ideas. Unfortunately, each pioneer customer usually has unique ideas about how to shape the innovation and makes demands that no one else would make. The market opportunity typically presented by these buyers is narrow and unpredictable.

Pragmatists

These buyers do not crave new products based on some larger vision of the future. They believe in evolutionary change rather than revolutionary change. They are, however, interested in making fundamental changes if doing so will make their lives better. They seek to adopt innovations only after a track record of performance has been established. References from people they trust are important. When they decide to adopt the new technology, they do so quickly and completely in order to make a clean break and to build all future efforts on the new paradigm. They prefer to buy from the perceived industry leader, not because of superior technical qualifications but because they believe the rest of the world will build to this standard and therefore make their investment more durable.

The nature of the business opportunity presented by this class buyer is narrowly focused. This class can be large enough for you to focus on the single best implementation of your innovation and still experience rapid growth.

Conservatives

These buyers are pessimistic about achieving significant benefit from a new product or service and will buy only after the trend toward its use is clear and well established. This is a large class of buyer, and competition for their spending can be intense. While the pragmatists established the product as the standard, the conservatives work the innovation into their existing buying habits. If they become customers, they become lasting customers. They are price sensitive, skeptical, and very demanding on issues of quality and reliability. They will consider competing products carefully. Although conservatives tend to have complex needs, their interest in going with established practices makes their demands predictable.

The business opportunity is immense and long-lasting but challenging. Their insistence that your innovation fit in seamlessly with their existing lives presents many challenges to overcome. But what they demand is usually stable over time, and your investment in meeting their needs can pay off over the long run.

Sophisticates

These buyers occupy niche situations for which standardized products are a poor fit, or they have changing needs which make them leery of big purchases. In both cases, they require personal attention and advice that will coax them into buying. They believe they have unique demands and are willing to pay a premium for products or services that meet these needs. This makes them sophisticates in terms of what they look for in a product or service. The business opportunity presented by sophisticates is also large, but it is more varied from segment to segment and changeable over time.

Laggards

This is a small class of buyers with varied reasons for being last to adopt the new product or technology. In general, the business opportunity presented by this class of buyer is small and can be disregarded in favor of the opportunities presented by others.

Phases of Business Development and Modes of Operation

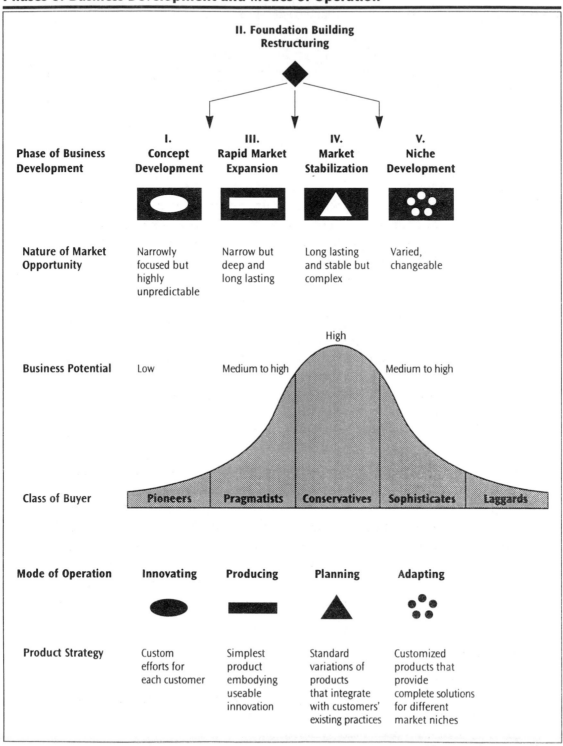

		II. Foundation Building Restructuring		
Phase of Business Development	**I. Concept Development**	**III. Rapid Market Expansion**	**IV. Market Stabilization**	**V. Niche Development**
Nature of Market Opportunity	Narrowly focused but highly unpredictable	Narrow but deep and long lasting	Long lasting and stable but complex	Varied, changeable
Business Potential	Low	Medium to high	High	Medium to high
Class of Buyer	Pioneers	Pragmatists	Conservatives	Sophisticates · Laggards
Mode of Operation	Innovating	Producing	Planning	Adapting
Product Strategy	Custom efforts for each customer	Simplest product embodying useable innovation	Standard variations of products that integrate with customers' existing practices	Customized products that provide complete solutions for different market niches

Impact of Buyer Classes

The classes of customers with the greatest business potential are the pragmatists, conservatives, and sophisticates. The pioneers are a small class of buyer but are important because they get you started. The laggards represent insignificant business potential. The Phases of Business Development and Modes of Operation chart shows how the classes of buyers correspond to the phases of development.

A change in the class of buyer does not always keep pace with changes in the phase of business development. This is especially true for the Foundation Building phase. This phase of development occurs while you are still serving the pioneers and has little to do with changes in market opportunity. As stated earlier, its focus is two-fold: to standardize what you are already doing intuitively so others can help support your vision and to lay the foundation for future growth in reaching the next classes of buyers.

The Road Map

The phases of your business are like different regions in the territory. A detailed road map shows several routes to various locations, and few of them are laid out in straight linear fashion. Similarly in business, your purpose is not just to take one straight line to some end destination and then stop. Your business is evolving and changing, so your path through the phases of business can take different directions and follow varying sequences. It is a development process that never ends.

The diagram on the following page is one of two versions of the *Surviving Success* road map for business growth and development. A more detailed version is introduced later in the book.

The four corner boxes represent the phases of business growth that generate business momentum. These momentum-building phases are periods of evolutionary growth when growth is achieved by doing more of what you are already doing. The center mode is a period of revolutionary change within the organization that prepares it for the next phase of development. This mode consumes business momentum.

The arrows show that you should not move directly from one corner box, momentum-building phase, to another. Instead, you should anticipate the change and navigate your organization through a transitional phase of restructuring to adequately prepare for the next momentum-building phase. During the Restructuring mode you will dismantle old structures and practices and lay the foundation for the next mode of operation.

Road Map – Version 1

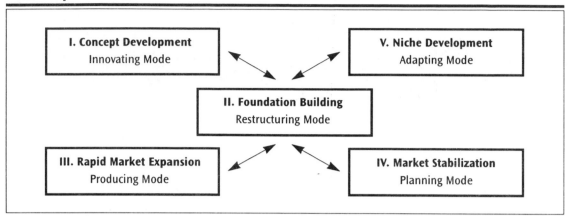

Many organizations will pass through the phases in the sequence indicated on the road map: I, II, III, IV, V. Although the sequence of modes can be different for different firms, you should strive to use the sequence that takes fullest advantage of market opportunities and provides your company with the broadest range of capabilities.

If your organization successfully meets the objectives of each phase, you will make maximum use of its capabilities and achieve full business potential. You will be ready to move on to the next phase of development, carrying along the beneficial legacies of all prior phases. In reality, these modes are interconnected rather than completely distinct and separate modes, but it is helpful to discuss them as distinct modes to fully understand the characteristic features of each.

The main point is to make sure you are attempting the right mode in the right situation. For example, improving the organization's efficiency in handling a complex manufacturing process may be the key to success during one period. Developing a breakthrough innovation may be the key in another. Training staff for more responsibility may be the most important issue for the company at another time.

Phases Change Independently but Modes Do Not

The market opportunities change and so should how you respond to them. While market opportunities can change independently of management effort, such as when one customer segment becomes saturated or competition steps into view, creating the modes of operation to exploit the opportunities requires significant effort.

There is nothing automatic about a transition of one mode of operation to the next. That is why it's important to grasp the distinctions between each phase and mode. You may, for example, have the opportunity for rapid market expansion but may or may not operate in a way that takes advantage of the situation.

Leaders who recognize the need for different modes of operation during different phases of their business's growth can set the priorities that lead to the creation of appropriate modes. Once you can identify the modes that are right for the different parts of your business, you can set out to build them. Even if a particular mode is not a good fit with your personal style and interests, you as the leader can consciously decide to create the needed mode by using other staff and by adopting specific disciplines.

Chapter 3

Management Styles

Management Styles Are Based on Personal Decision Styles

Personal Decision Styles

Master the Art of the Appropriate Response

Chapter 3

Management Styles

Your personal management style has great impact on the business strategies you select as well as on the structure, culture, and priorities of your organization. Unless there is conscious effort to do otherwise, your management style can determine your organization's entire mode of operation.

Since a small or rapidly growing business rarely has formal organizational and business strategies in place, these strategies grow naturally from the leader's personal management style. The direction you favor as leader is often the direction your company takes. The leader's management style often becomes the benchmark for determining if others are behaving as needed. If a leader values spontaneity, for example, then spontaneous people are often viewed favorably. If a leader does thorough research before making a decision, others try to follow suit. Your management style therefore has tremendous impact on the strategic direction of the firm and its daily operation.

If you know your natural preferences and what is required to be effective in a particular situation, you can consciously change your priorities and behavior. Even if you cannot make all the required changes personally, your intelligent and effective use of other people can provide your business much of what it needs.

Management Styles Are Based on Personal Decision Styles

There are five different management styles associated with the five modes of operation listed in the prior section. They are included under the modes of operation in the Management Styles for Leaders chart.

Management Styles for Leaders

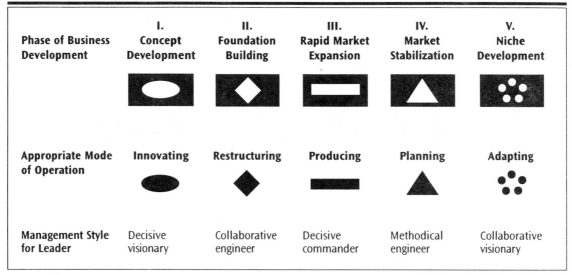

	I. Concept Development	II. Foundation Building	III. Rapid Market Expansion	IV. Market Stabilization	V. Niche Development
Phase of Business Development					
Appropriate Mode of Operation	Innovating	Restructuring	Producing	Planning	Adapting
Management Style for Leader	Decisive visionary	Collaborative engineer	Decisive commander	Methodical engineer	Collaborative visionary

These management styles represent various preferences for different ways of making decisions in management situations. Broadly speaking, people manage others the same way they make decisions for themselves. You can assess certain elements of your management style by measuring your personal decision style.

Personal decision-making preferences can be measured easily and objectively using various standard tests and tools, such as the Decision Style Inventory, developed of Dr. Alan J. Rowe, which is included in Appendix A. Take a moment now to take the test and determine your preferences. Identifying your personal decision style now before reading the rest of the book will help you get much more out of the material. Another test measuring similar characteristics is the Myers Briggs Type Indicator.

Personal Decision Styles

Decision style characterizes the way you prefer to work with people, information, and tasks to make and implement decisions. Personal decision styles influence the way you perceive problems and the types of solutions you seek. Although everyone displays aspects of each of these four styles, for most people there is a dominant style. The next most preferred style, the back-up style, is typically used when you reach an impasse in using the dominant style.

The four personal decision styles are:

- Directive
- Analytic
- Conceptual
- Behavioral

Each of Dr. Rowe's four personal decision styles are summarized below.

Directive

The directive decision style is characterized by its emphasis on the here and now. Directive individuals tend to make decisions quickly and consider only specific, objective facts. Their priority is to get the job done. They are action oriented and decisive and look for speed, efficiency, and results. They like short reports with summarized conclusions, tend to have many people reporting to them, and maintain tight control of the decision-making process. They tend to control others through supervision. People with a directive style can be autocratic and readily exercise their power and control. They sometimes feel insecure and want status to protect their positions.

The strength of this style is that directive individuals can quickly mobilize resources to meet specific task-oriented objectives. The weakness of this style is that directive individuals behave as if they expect the future to be a repeat of the past; they do very little formal or informal long-term planning.

Analytic

Analytic individuals tend to seek the best-supported solution to problems based on a defensible and logical organization of the facts. They make decisions only after reviewing the facts. People with this style see the technical aspects of situations and enjoy solving complex problems. They enjoy searching for complete, accurate facts and carefully studying the facts to see what possibilities exist. They tend to like long written reports and are most comfortable taking action after the decision and all its implications have been clearly defined. People with an analytic style can often be highly autocratic. They place high priority on using rules and procedures to control others and like well-defined organizational structures.

Highly analytic people are good at solving complex problems, conducting thorough research, and following detailed plans. The drawback to this style is the potential for analysis paralysis, an endless cycle of studies and reports. There is a tendency to over-analyze a situation in the search for the best possible solution.

Conceptual

The conceptual style of decision making is characterized by creativity and a big-picture perspective. Conceptual individuals seek something larger than the best solution; they seek universal truth. They habitually scan the horizon for opportunities and threats. They are intuitive in their decision making; they make the decision first and then gather information to support or challenge their decision. These individuals are flexible, curious, and open-minded. They want independence and dislike following rules. Conceptual people are perfectionists especially concerning their vision, want to see many options, and are concerned about the future. They are creative in finding answers to problems and can easily visualize future alternatives and consequences. They have a high commitment to their organizations and value praise, recognition, and independence. They prefer loose control and are willing to share power. Communication is open and wide ranging.

Strengths of this style are creativity and vision. Conceptual individuals can see broad realities that are not apparent to others. A weakness of this style is the tendency to look for new solutions when current ones are sufficient. Also, they can rely too much on intuition and feelings.

Behavioral

The behavioral style is the most people oriented of all four decision styles. Behavioral individuals are sensitive to and consider the views of others when making decisions. They can be political in their approach to problems and can quickly identify the common bonds among people that create coalitions. People with a behavioral style also are supportive, are sensitive to suggestions, show warmth, use persuasion to influence others, accept loose formal controls, and prefer verbal to written reports. They tend to focus on short-run problems and are action oriented. They want acceptance and care deeply about the organization and the development of its people. Behavioral people tend to rely on meetings to exchange information, to develop a consensus, and to serve as an important part of the decision process. Achieving understanding, agreement, consensus, and a positive working environment are important priorities.

The strength of the behavioral style is the ability to create common understanding and consensus. Listening and empathy are often key attributes of leaders with this style.

The weakness of this approach is that decision making can be time consuming and often requires the presence of other people knowledgeable in relevant matters.

The Personal Decision Styles Underlying Management Styles chart shows how the personal decision styles correspond to the five management styles, modes, and phases.

Personal Decision Styles Underlying Management Styles

	I. Concept Development	II. Foundation Building	III. Rapid Market Expansion	IV. Market Stabilization	V. Niche Development
Phase of Business Development					
Appropriate Mode of Operation	Innovating	Restructuring	Producing	Planning	Adapting
Management Style for Leader	Decisive visionary	Collaborative engineer	Decisive commander	Methodical engineer	Collaborative visionary
Personal Decision Style	Conceptual, low analytic, with directive as backup	Analytic and behavioral	Highly directive	Highly analytic	Conceptual with behavioral as backup

The decisive visionary management style is characteristic of someone who, compared to the average person, is highly conceptual, is not very analytic, and uses directive as the main back-up style. The collaborative engineer is characteristic of one who is highly analytic and highly behavioral, compared to the average population. The methodical engineer is highly analytic. The collaborative visionary is characteristic of one who is conceptual with a strong element of behavioral.

Leaders with the management styles indicated above are the naturally most effective leaders of the respective modes of operation; that is, they find those modes to be the most pleasant and comfortable. If these leaders build an organization consistent with their personal preferences, they will create, almost spontaneously, something similar to the modes indicated above.

Just as the Concept Development phase is most effectively exploited with the Innovating mode of operation, innovation is most effectively managed by a decisive visionary, a leader who is creative and has an action orientation.

The Foundation Building phase is most effectively exploited with the Restructuring mode of operation. In turn, the Restructuring mode is most effectively managed by a collaborative engineer, a leader who seeks the views of others, bases decisions on objective information, and establishes predictable plans and strategies.

The Rapid Market Expansion phase is most effectively exploited with the Producing mode of operation. The Producing mode is most effectively managed by a decisive commander, a leader who identifies specific, task-oriented objectives and has an action orientation.

The Market Stabilization phase is most effectively exploited with the Planning mode of operation. Planning is most effectively managed by a methodical engineer, a leader who gathers a wide range of information before making decisions and engineers detailed long-term plans and strategies.

The Niche Development phase is most effectively exploited with the Adapting mode of operation. In turn, the Adapting mode is most effectively managed by a collaborative visionary, a leader who is creative, cares deeply about the human element of the business, and actively solicits information and opinions.

It is important to note what is not indicated by these personal decision styles and the management styles they create. While they describe an individual's preferences and personal priorities, they do not measure wisdom, intelligence, ambition, motivation, or energy, all of which are vital ingredients to success. What they do indicate is who will be most comfortable in each mode and phase.

There is no guarantee that, for example, all decisive visionaries will be good at creating innovations for your company. Not all decisive visionaries will automatically select the right strategies, pursue the appropriate actions, nor create the right decision structures.

Road Map – Version 1 with Management Styles

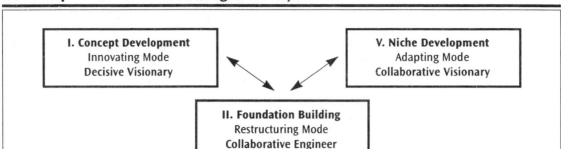

The naturally most effective management styles have been added to the Road Map.

With the addition of the naturally most effective management styles, the terrain described by the road map becomes more vivid. You can infer more about the nature of the phases from the types of leaders who are effective in those situations.

The boxes in the left half of the diagram are the modes that depend on the leader's personal handling of key issues. Those on the right half of the map indicate modes that depend more on the leader working through the organization's people or policies to achieve success. The top half of the diagram indicates modes that depend most on individuals being thoroughly knowledgeable of the main issues confronting the organization. The bottom half indicates modes that depend relatively more on operational efficiency for success.

Thus, the Innovating mode requires the leader and organization to have a thorough understanding of the issues and to be directly involved with key decisions.

The Producing mode is also a hands-on phase but depends more on operational efficiency than in-depth knowledge of the issues.

The Planning mode requires operational efficiency and the ability to work through other people and the organization's policies.

The Adapting mode requires that many staff have complete understanding of their market segments and that the leader have the ability to work through and motivate others.

Master the Art of the Appropriate Response

You are probably familiar with tests that indicate your aptitude and preference for certain professions. You may have taken a test that indicates you are best suited to being a flight attendant, a surgeon, or an architect. The key to happiness, the logic goes, is to seek the profession for which you are best suited. This strategy is fine for stable professions, but the profession of leading a small or rapidly growing business organization defies a simple classification. There is no one single set of aptitudes and personal decision styles that is well suited to all the situations you will encounter as your business grows and matures. Stated more simply, the job of the leader changes as the business grows.

Striving to make the job of leader fit your personal preferences will either hinder the growth of the business or cause you significant personal discomfort. Most likely, both will occur. Thus, in response to the different phases of your business's development, you and your organization must both evolve and create a mode of operation that is best suited to the situation.

When you take on the role of an entrepreneur, you step forward to be exposed to all different types of situations; some will match what interests you, some will not. The names of the modes describe the scope of priorities the leader will have to champion through each mode: innovating, restructuring, producing, planning, and adapting. The central issue for the entrepreneurial leader is to master the art of the appropriate response.

As the creative leader, owner, and business manager, the entrepreneurial leader confronts it all, incidental issues, people problems, and technical problems requiring great creativity or extensive research, all aspects of the real world. The leader must see the problems for what they are in cold reality and respond in ways that address the most important issues and effectively move the business forward. You cannot be successful over the long term in a growing business by being a solution looking for problems. The problems force themselves on you, and your cannot be selective about which ones you will address and which ones you leave unattended.

Yet few organizations progress smoothly from one mode of successful growth to the next. Transitions are difficult because dramatic change is required to move from one mode to the next. In addition, there is no naturally occurring force that causes the new mode of operation to appear. A deliberate confluence of efforts, intentions, and forces is needed to shift to another mode. Unlike the development of human beings, who mature from childhood into adolescence because of genetic programming, a business requires conscious choice and action to create the right mode at the right time. It also requires wisdom and the strength to overcome the natural tendency to avoid change and take paths of least resistance.

Fortunately, there are indicators that change is due. There are symptoms that the organizational structure, culture, and management priorities have been preserved beyond their usefulness and are out of alignment with the requirements of the current business situation. This misalignment is the result of undesirable legacies left from past successes. They indicate that you are off track and need to rethink the direction of your business and organization. As symptoms, some may not be critical by themselves, but as indicators of deeper problems, you should watch for them and take them seriously when they arise.

You as a leader can identify the various road blocks that are put in place by successful innovation before they detour you completely. The next several chapters will detail the phases of development, modes of operation, and classic legacies of each mode. With this information, you will have the tools and information you need to provide the most effective leadership you can and to successfully guide your organization through a smooth developmental path.

Chapter 4

Breaking New Ground

Chapter 4

Breaking New Ground

What an exciting time this is to be part of the team. Everything is new, fresh, and invigorating, a thrill ride every day. The Concept Development phase and its Innovating mode of operation embody the excitement, exhilaration, and intensity of bringing a new idea into the world.

However, this phase of development fulfills just half of the dream of starting one's own business. Unfortunately, unbeknownst to most who start new businesses, the other half of the dream, business success, comes not from this phase but from later phases. The fact that this phase is just a phase in a larger progression is indeed a surprise to most entrepreneurs.

Carl, the highly creative entrepreneurial leader introduced earlier, is taking his business through the Concept Development phase. Although this is the third time Carl is experiencing this phase, he too feels the fresh beginning.

The Thrill of Innovation

MaxCo, a large, highly visible manufacturing company and key customer for Carl's Model 2000, had great respect for Carl's expertise. They had called him in to fix a machine unrelated to the Model

2000. Downtime caused by the failure was costing them thousands of dollars a day.

It was just after the Christmas toy season, and Carl realized that the problem could be solved by using the same type of mechanism that spins the rotor on his son's toy helicopter. Carl read up on helicopter mechanics for two days and went to work designing a new part.

Carl called his team into the shop over the weekend to craft a prototype for MaxCo's new part. He was like a fire horse after hearing the alarm. Adrenaline was flowing and the creative energy was at its peak. He was in his element as he spilled out diagrams across the white board, spoke passionately about the possibilities, and convinced the team that they could work miracles.

For this new innovation, his hand-selected team consisted of six key members. Four had been with Carl for three years and had experienced the prior innovations. Two had been hired over the prior 18 months.

Oddly, the staff designers largely responsible for the development of the Model 2000 were cut out of the MaxCo project entirely. Carl wanted the prototype made now and believed the regular design process would simply take too much time. He also believed that it would not be possible to articulate his vision to the staff designers quickly and completely enough because he did not have a formal design for the prototype; it was in his head. He alone knew the broken machine, why the customer had the problem, and how the solution could be found in helicopter technology. Besides, Carl was an expert designer and machinist, so if anyone could design and supervise construction at the same time, he could.

The team worked diligently over the weekend. During the long hours, Carl moved around the shop hovering over team members to make sure each part was being crafted to fit with every other part. When a fit wasn't quite right, Carl would indicate the adjustments required. All jobs were shared so that when one team member finished the piece they were working on, they would work on another.

By the end of the weekend they had a successfully working prototype based on helicopter technology. Early Monday morning, Carl asked the staff designers, who were smarting a bit from being left out, to identify critical weaknesses in the prototype before Carl showed it to MaxCo that afternoon.

MaxCo staff looked at the machine and immediately saw its potential, not only to address their current problem but also for other key applications. So did Carl. And thus was born the Model 3000.

The Concept Development Phase

You have a concept for a breakthrough innovation and perhaps a thought of who could benefit from your idea. However, neither of these ideas has been tested or validated. At this point, there is no guarantee that you have a valuable product or that a market exists that is large enough to make it worthwhile to make and sell the product.

Your market during this Concept Development phase is not really a market yet. It is a collection of pioneering customers willing to give you an opportunity to fulfill their visions of the potential for your idea. They like new ideas and have their own vision of what you can do for them. They are willing to give you this opportunity on the chance that it addresses a chronically unmet need. They recognize it may not work and will want a significant price discount. In addition, these trendsetters will ask for special features that no one else will ask for.

Now is your opportunity to work with these visionary customers who are willing to give you a chance. Learn from the information they provide you. The lessons will be valuable both immediately and later.

Survival and Validation

During concept development, the most pressing issues facing your fledgling business are surviving, validating your concept, translating the concept into a product or service, and assessing its marketability.

Survival and validating the concept and its marketability are center stage. They are so fundamental to the existence of the firm that they deserve the level of intense focus commonly associated with a crisis. Yet they are issues that defy being reduced formulae and plans.

Late nights and unpredictable workflow are simply part of the business during this phase. The need to pay the bills and to invest in the development of the product pushes many other issues into the background. The firm does not have the luxury of worrying about the fine points of such things as compensation schemes, accounting systems, and formal internal controls.

Your mission is to develop a successful breakthrough innovation, one that is so attractive that it will dramatically change the spending habits of a large number of buyers and propel the firm forward in business. This could be the beginning of your business, or you could be entering this mode in an effort to rejuvenate an existing business. In either case, the situation is the same, and you seek to break new ground.

Suppose you believe that your innovation will ultimately work, but there is little evidence to support this claim. While it is in the concept stage, you must discover what form it will actually take. This is largely a trial-and-error discovery process. Validation may involve working out some of the final technical details of the innovation in order to make sure that it actually works. Validation might also involve introducing a new product in the marketplace or placing an existing product in a new market.

The Innovating Mode of Operation

Typical themes of an innovating organization are:

- Build a better mousetrap and the world will beat a path to your door.
- If you are not going to do it right, don't do it.
- This innovation will rewrite the rules of the industry.
- Everything matters.

These themes reflect an arrogance and boldness characteristic of many entrepreneurial leaders who are driven by an ambition to change the world or at least a meaningful part of it. While few ultimately fulfill such lofty objectives, their desire to do so propels them and their businesses far into the business world. Some may say these start-up entrepreneurs are fooling themselves and others by aiming so high and imply that they should not. It might be more realistic to view these ambitions more like the nuclear fuel that drives a reactor — dangerous if poorly channeled and directed but the source of immense value if the energy can be harnessed safely.

Management Style – Decisive Visionary

During the Innovating mode, the most naturally effective management style is decisive visionary, which has conceptual as the dominant decision style, with directive as the backup. To an extent, this style is simply the package that the breakthrough ideas come in. The research for this book suggests that the CEOs of successful venture capital funded companies who developed the concept on which the company was founded were decisive visionaries. As conceptual thinkers, they tend to be highly intuitive and creative and use their broad, integrated vision to identify new ways to solve problems. They often make decisions first and then gather information to support the idea. Creative ideas alone, however, are not sufficient in the Innovation mode. Creativity should be tempered with having a keen interest in putting the ideas into action, which is characteristic of the directive decision style.

These decisive visionaries are most comfortable with small, informally-structured groups of people. They like the hands-on, quick-moving nature of the Innovating mode of operation. They value loyalty and commitment in their employees and prefer to have direct interaction with all the staff. They get data and impressions from the staff, but the leader makes all decisions. Because they tend to be highly energetic and focused on a narrow set of issues, they readily absorb all relevant information about their primary interest.

Most Effective Structure

The most effective organizational structure for innovation is a tribe of focused generalists. This structure is highly centralized and informal. Everyone participates in all decisions, but the leader makes essentially all final decisions. Everyone in the small organization is tuned to the vision of the leader, and they depend on the leader's vision for daily guidance. This structure is diagrammed as follows, with the leader indicated by a square and employees as circles.

There is little specialization of work, with each person performing a variety of functions. All members of the team work together, pitching in to do whatever is needed to move forward, often forsaking personal comfort and security. One day the whole team might be testing the product in the shop, and the next day everyone could be talking to prospective customers.

This flexible structure enables the leader to ensure that every move is consistent with the path unfolding before them. After taking a few steps, the leader may discover that the path he or she selected will not work, and they must backtrack and try another. Cohesiveness and responsiveness of the small group are crucial to moving through the discovery process, and the more quickly the small team can change direction, the better.

The constant contact between the leader and the rest of the staff enables the organization to quickly and easily refine everyone's short- and long-term objectives and make mid-course corrections to the overall strategy. Delegation is not an issue because everyone works together to get the job done.

The number of people involved in the organization, usually less than 10 people, is small enough that all involved can sit around a table and discuss the issues of the day. Everyone must know what everyone else is thinking and doing in order to make instantaneous changes in their activities. Little is written down because everyone is there to hear and understand all discussions. The emphasis is on teamwork and innovation, and almost every problem receives the full attention of the whole team.

Decision making may feel collaborative because everyone is involved in all decisions, but, in fact, the leader is the main and perhaps singular decision maker. Other people are used as extensions of the leader's data-gathering and processing abilities, essentially feeding information to the leader for the final decision. Everyone votes, but only one vote counts. Although there is a feeling of consensus, the leader plays the crucial role of calling a close to the discussion and asserting the decision.

Controlling an Innovating Organization

Initially, the leader personally and directly controls the activities of members of the organization. Of course, as the organization grows, it is not possible nor advisable for the leader to personally control all activities.

Methods of Control

Direct personal interaction and supervision by the leader	Personally guiding and supervising others' activities.
Business vision	Establishing a compelling and loyalty-inspiring business vision indicating the appropriate direction for the organization.
Cultural priorities	Formally and informally emphasizing the importance of certain issues.
Organizational hierarchy	Encouraging others to follow the guidance of people higher up the chain of command.
Formal rules and strategies	Establishing clear plans, policies, instructions, and rules for team and individual actions and how those actions relate to those of other teams and individuals.
Expertise of individual members	Allowing members to use their own discretion to determine the best course of action.
Formal evaluation and feedback	Providing comment and feedback regarding their past performance to enable the individuals to self-correct their actions.

Direct control must be replaced with other, intermediate forms of control that the leader can use to indirectly influence others. The direct and intermediate controls are listed in the Methods of Control chart.

Problems arise when the intermediate controls needed for the next mode of operation are inadequate. The organization then begins to be out of control, and the leader often reasserts the controls effective during a past mode of operation. Development ceases, regardless of how the external business opportunities change.

The types of controls used by the organization are, along with the organizational structure, management, and cultural priorities, a key characteristic of each mode of operation. A profile of controls characteristic of the Innovating mode are shown in the Profile of Control Methods chart. The control profile indicates the relative importance or weight of each control. The higher the weight, the more important the control is as a way of influencing the activities of the organization's members.

In an innovating organization, control is maintained primarily through direct interaction of all members of the organization with the leader and the use of a loyalty-inspiring vision. The day-to-day, direct interaction with the leader ensures that the efforts of every member of the organization are coordinated and appropriate for the issues at hand. This form of supervision is so effective that the entire organization often can change direction almost instantaneously.

The loyalty-inspiring vision proactively ensures that the individual decisions made by the organization's members are compatible. Even

Profile of Control Methods

Phase of Business Development	Concept Development
Mode of Operation	Innovating
Important Controls	Supervision, vision
Control Profiles	**Relative Weight**
Direct personal interaction and supervision	60
Business vision	25
Cultural priorities	5
Organizational hierarchy	0
Formal rules and strategies	0
Expertise of individual members	10
Formal evaluation and feedback	0
Total weight	100%

though the business situations change quickly in the first phase of development, each individual member of the organization can determine how to make decisions in a way compatible with the vision.

Loyalty is such an important element of control and cultural feature of innovating organizations that loyalty betrayed or abandoned is almost a capital offense. Other forms of control, such as rules, procedures, monitoring, and feedback, are not needed and are, in fact, less responsive and effective for controlling the output of this small team.

The Product Is Customized for Each Customer

During the Innovating mode, your product is a custom effort for anyone willing to give it a try. You become completely involved with the customer's thinking, emotions, and situations in order to think through what they need and want.

They need not be able to articulate what they want because you are there to think it through with them. Familiarity is a key. You need to know their situation better, or at least from a valuable new perspective, than they know it themselves. When you have a sense of what might work for them, give it a try, and see if it fulfills your vision of what should happen. If it does, go through the same process with another prospective buyer. If not, revise the effort and try again.

Try various customers with different needs. Provide all the benefits they articulate as well as those they do not, and study their reactions. Evaluate how easily generalized your product is.

The Concept Development Summary chart summarizes the key features of the Concept Development phase and the Innovating mode of operation.

Features of Interest

Of all that takes place in the Concept Development phase, a few of the most interesting and important features are described next. These features are interesting now, but, as you will later learn, they lead to challenges you must face in the future.

Defiant Innovation

Successful innovating organizations typically have in their culture a certain contempt for the current activities in the marketplace. There is the sense that the customers do not really know yet what they truly need or want. The operating belief is often that the visionary leader has identified

Concept Development Summary

Phase of Business Development	Concept Development
Critical Objectives	• Creation of breakthrough innovation. • Survival of the organization. • Validation of business and product concepts.
Appropriate Mode of Operation	Innovating
Typical Themes	• Build a better mousetrap and the world will beat a path to your door. • If you are not going to do it right, don't do it. • This innovation will rewrite the rules of the industry. • Everything matters.
Most Effective Organizational Structure	Team of focused generalists. Few rules or procedures. Everyone is involved with every decision. Although often dominant, the central leader can be egalitarian.
Cultural Priorities	• Insight and new ideas. • Agility and action. • Informal decision making. • Customized work. • Defiance of conventional wisdom.
Important Controls	• Direct personal interaction and supervision. • Loyalty-inspiring vision.
Naturally Most Effective Management Style for the Leader	Decisive visionary. Highly conceptual, low analytic, with directive as a backup.
Prerequisites	• Less than 10 people involved in decision making, because of its being a new organization or a conscious choice to limit the size of the group. • A small number of overriding issues that command the attention of the team, with no critical need to attend to others, due to there being a dominant critical issue or a conscious choice to limit the complexity of the management situation. • Direct contact between the decision makers and the environment; people are not insulated from external information.

a need of the market that has not yet been articulated by the marketplace itself. If the company can fill the need before others do, the business benefits are tremendous.

Because the vision is often bold and far-reaching, there is a feeling that the industry and potential competitors are not likely to be doing anything of value. This makes it seem a waste of time and effort to keep up with what other companies are doing.

Defiance of the conventional wisdom of the marketplace enables an organization to pursue its independent path without being swayed by the existing industry situation. Defiant innovation is, in this situation, a benefit that enables you to pursue a dramatically new view of the world.

Loyalty Contributes to Agility

During the trial-and-error process of discovery, effective leaders typically populate their organizations with energetic and loyal implementors rather than with independent, visionary decision makers. This is because members insisting upon being completely independent decision makers often introduce more distraction than strength during this phase. Their independence from the vision of the leader prevents them from keeping up with the day-to-day refinement of the strategy. Thus the focus and resources of the organization would be diluted.

Energy, loyalty, and dutiful implementation of instructions therefore become more important qualities than an ability to strategize or to make decisions independently. Also, people with generalist skills or interests are sought because they need to play a variety of roles. Of course, the new entrepreneur often simply takes whoever is available, friends, relatives, and neighbors, for this initial phase.

Accountabilities Are Irrelevant

The generalist nature of the staff, having everyone involved in every effort and decision, and the leader's close supervision of the entire trial-and-error process make it unimportant to formally determine who has final accountability for any decision. The leader is accountable for all decisions. Failure and mistakes by anyone in the organization are attributed to the team and the leader.

The Need for a Singular Vision

Having a singular vision during the Innovating mode is extremely important. Because decision making and planning are informal and intuitive at this stage, an organization with multiple, competing visions wastes precious resources trying to consolidate them. For this reason, it is often best to follow essentially one visionary through the process of developing and refining a concept. The benefits of following a single visionary are so great that there is a discernible effect within successful Innovating organizations that can be called leadership allelopathy.

Allelopathy (pronounced al-lee'-lo-pathy) is a term borrowed from the field of biology referring to the growth-inhibiting influence of one living plant upon another. Some species of plants have evolved over time to possess a capability that helps promote the success of the species. When one individual of a species with allelopathic capabilities germinates, it emits toxins into the air and soil that inhibit the normal development of other seedlings of its same species. Thus, other seedlings sprouting later are stunted in their development, and the first seedling is allowed to become the dominant individual.

Once the dominant individual is well established, it stops emitting the toxins, and the other seedlings resume normal growth, albeit a step behind the dominant individual. The species benefits from reduced competition for water or minerals that may be scarce in the area. Should these resources be depleted, the larger, better established individual has a greater chance of maturing enough to produce seeds for the next generation. Without the allelopathic effect, the entire population of equally developed individuals may perish during a period of depleted resources.

A similar effect is found in successful innovating organizations. The dominant leader undermines others in order to remain dominant or to become more dominant. Dominant does not necessarily mean domineering. It simply means that decision making is guided and coordinated by that individual person. Multiple visionaries can be accommodated within the organization if one is clearly dominant by virtue of age, personality, or some other feature that prevents direct competition.

Even team members who are not competing visionaries are affected by leadership allelopathy. Visionary leaders tend to avoid other independent thinkers and hire individuals who can be loyal to the leader's vision. The organization's culture, decision-making structure, and compensation practices often encourage loyalty to the leader's view. With only one real decision maker in an innovating organization, the other members are not given the chance to develop as independent decision makers. These forces are often so powerful that even people who would otherwise be independent thinkers and doers do not develop those characteristics. They are encouraged and rewarded for respecting the dominance of the leader.

Another factor that contributes to leadership allelopathy is the intuitive aspect of the leader's decisive visionary management style. The members of the organization must pay close attention in order to track their leader's moves. The thought processes and actions of such leaders are not linear and predictable and are therefore not easily tracked. One moment they are thinking and talking about one subject and then instantaneously shifting to another, leaving the staff to mentally scamper to the new position.

It is like hunting for grouse with a bird dog in tall grass. The leader is like the highly sensitive dog sniffing out the game. One moment the grass rustles on the left, the next on the right. When the dog finds game, it flushes it out of the brush. The task of the hunter is not to find the game but to track the dog. It quickly becomes clear that tracking the dog is more effective for the hunter than trying to locate the grouse. This system works for all as long as the dog stays interested and involved. If the dog is taken out of the picture, the hunter will find that he is ill-prepared to find game on his own. Similarly, the staff of an innovating organization focus more on predicting what the leader will do next rather than what the market will do next.

Even if the decisive visionary leader pulls back on the allelopathic effect, the fact that it has taken place sets the stage for future issues. Typically, the decisive visionary hires loyal implementors with generalist skills. The loyal implementors in turn hire people highly skilled in narrow fields of expertise.

Common Errors

Like the plants with allelopathic traits, the visionary leader must manage their dominance. Once the business is established, staff should be trained to read the market — or hunt grouse — on their own. Otherwise successful leaders will often make two errors in this regard; either they give up their dominant role too soon or they refuse to give it up when they should.

A leader should consider retaining the dominant role while the organization still fits the conditions of an Innovating mode of operation, which are:

- Less than 10 people involved in decision making, either because of its being a new organization or a conscious choice to limit the size of the group.
- A small number of overriding issues that command the attention of the team, with no critical need to attend to others, due to there being a dominant critical issue or a conscious choice to limit the complexity of the management situation.

- Direct contact between the decision makers and the environment so that people are not insulated from external information.

When these prerequisites are still valid, the Innovating mode remains the ideal mode of operation.

In some investment management firms, for example, a star investor may have several research analysts to provide support. As these research analysts progress in their careers, they begin to seek larger roles in decision making. If they are given a larger role when the situation still fits the conditions noted above, the singular vision embodied in the investment process begins to fragment. When this happens, unless other steps are taken, investment performance deteriorates. In such cases, the business is better off if the leader maintains the dominant role. Although it may seem unfair to constrain the career aspirations of the staff, it may be in the long-term best interest of the business for one individual to provide a singular focus for vision and decisions.

However, as your business begins to grow beyond the capacities of an Innovating organization, it is less appropriate, and even unwise, for the leader to dominate decision making.

The second error leaders commonly make during this time is to become accustomed to the dominant role and refuse to give it up when they should. People like the power of the dominant role, and because it has been effective, they feel justified in maintaining it. They are also afraid of losing control of what has been essentially their creation. When the business situation changes, the organization should move on to the Restructuring mode to prepare for the future.

Look for these indications that your firm is moving out of the Innovating mode:

- Validating a breakthrough innovation is no longer the most important objective.
- A wider variety of issues begins to command management attention.
- The market stabilizes, and useful objective information becomes more plentiful.
- The organization grows larger and begins to insulate the leader from the market environment.
- There are more people involved in decision making than can sit around one table.

Once these signs are apparent, the leader must lead the business and organization to another mode of successful operation.

Signs of Success

Once the vision has been validated in the marketplace, it's likely the Concept Development phase is coming to an end. Validation may mean the introduction and acceptance of your product or services, or it may simply mean that the breakthrough technology has been proven to work. In either case, the question of whether or not the venture has a reason to exist fades in importance.

After validation of the basic vision, survival is no longer the major issue. Other issues begin to emerge. Subgroups form within your organization, and their agendas begin to develop independently of the leader. The organization no longer has a singular focus. These are the first clues that is it time to lay the foundation for future growth.

The important beneficial legacies of the Innovation mode are an impassioned and loyal staff, an initial taste of success, and a collection of customers who like your product. Your customers have tried your product and are willing to tell others about its benefits.

Limitations and Vulnerabilities

A critical limitation of an innovating organization is the number of people who can be effectively involved in the informal structure. Nine people should be considered the maximum. As the organization grows past those nine members, it will not have an effective centralized and informal structure because the leader cannot be personally involved in every detail of the organization on a daily basis. An organization of more than nine people usually requires a more structured way of making decisions.

If your business requires continual breakthrough innovation, don't grow. Stay with fewer than 10 people involved in decision making. Contract out as many other functions as possible, if needed, to stay within the capacity and capabilities of an Innovating organization.

There is a valuable example of this in the asset management business. In terms of investment performance, some asset management organizations have to make innovative investment decisions every month. They need continual breakthroughs. If they take their eyes off the ball, the effect is immediate, objective, and obvious: poor investment performance. Because of this fact of their business, they often limit the size of the decision-making groups or decision structures to fewer than ten people. This preserves flexibility, and yet it still remains an effective organization. Back-office activities, data processing, and other incidentals are contracted out to other organizations. Doing so reduces the number of issues the organization must contend with and prevents the decision makers from becoming isolated from the investment markets.

Carl's Model 3000

As Carl's team sat around the prototype of the Model 3000, they felt a mixture of exhaustion, euphoria, and trepidation. Like its predecessors, especially the Model 1000, the Model 3000 broke new ground and, they believed, set new standards for the industry.

Only the old-timers tempered their excitement. They had experienced the thrill of breakthrough innovation before and had seen that innovative ideas don't automatically guarantee industry leadership. Carl knew that their potential customers would not only have to find out about the Model 3000 but would also have to modify their own practices in order to use it. This created a high barrier to rapid adoption of the Model 3000 and to growth for the company. Staff who had joined Carl over the last 18 months, however, had boundless enthusiasm for the future.

Regardless of how they felt, they did have a new opportunity for growth and a shot at industry dominance. With existing sales of the Model 2000 combined with those for the Model 3000, they could grow with confidence.

Carl knew a shift in their thinking would soon be required. He prepared himself for the change and also began to signal to others that a phase was coming to an end. He encouraged everyone to celebrate their successes and how they produced those successes. He also encouraged them to talk openly about what they would have to do differently to continue to be successful.

The Transition

The transition from the Concept Development phase to the Foundation Building phase is often the most difficult transition. Everything that worked like a charm during concept development becomes a curse when building a foundation for future growth.

It was exciting to be part of an organization during Innovation. It was a time of collaboration and discovery, a time when all efforts were focused on developing and validating the vision. The leader and the other members of the organization identified at a personal level with the path they took during the Concept Development phase, regardless of how many unneeded bends and turns there were in the path. Their current success asserts that the path was ultimately effective so should be maintained. The path remains an important element in people's concept of who they are and the role they play in the organization. People become attached to the ways of the Innovating mode.

In addition, decisive visionaries are natural innovators, and leaders with this management style will understandably be uncomfortable when the focus shifts to building a foundation. Many are, therefore, reluctant to change. They see that what they enjoyed in the early days was effective and say, "Let's keep doing what works." If they do get a sense of the new direction ahead, they often reject it and say, "No way. Those are the reasons I left Big Bureaucracy, Inc., to form my own company." These feelings, while understandable, could torpedo the very success the enterprise is beginning to enjoy.

Don't overreact if you feel personally out of sync with the organization or as if you are missing external market opportunities as you begin to build infrastructure. If the breakthrough concept that you validated in the first phase is truly valuable and you restructure as soon as needed, the momentum of that idea and its success will carry you through the period of time it takes to restructure.

Turning your attention away from the market during this phase is particularly difficult for the breakthrough-oriented leader. It is boring for the innovative leader to build structures and have meetings. But if initiated when the decision-making organization has about ten people, the restructuring should not last long, and the firm can resume another mode of growth. Restructuring modes are temporary. When completed, it is time again to move on, and subsequent modes can be more interesting to the leader.

Undesirable Legacy

Some of the most trying problems a business can face are those rooted in practices that have been successful in the past. For a business that just experienced a successful Innovating mode, a common undesirable legacy is a reluctance to demystify the magic that created the breakthrough innovation and all its supporting activities.

Members of the organization feel good about the success of earlier efforts, and they develop a strong attachment to what they did to produce their successes. However, they view past successes as a function of their good judgment and experience and resist suggestions that they need to restructure and simplify what they do. Consequently, they think they have a complete understanding of the various steps they take to accomplish their work. Also, they believe that all steps they take have value, otherwise they would not be taking them. Neither is true.

Why It Is a Problem

Problems arise when decision making and work processes remain intuitive. When this happens, people are less able to make independent and rational decisions about how to improve the efficiency of what they do and how to involve other people meaningfully in decision making. If the individual elements of key practices are not clearly defined, it will be difficult to refine those practices to be more suitable for ongoing production. Training others in these practices will be impossible.

Without structured activities that enable a wider range of people to participate, effective delegation is not possible. People who have not grown up with the practices as they have evolved will rarely be effective in a reasonable amount of time. Leaders of the firm will have to devote a larger share of their time to internal issues.

How It Originated

This undesirable legacy is based on the intuitive decision making that is so successful in developing a breakthrough innovation. Intuitive decision making takes place within individuals as they assemble various cues and bits of information from a wide variety of sources and then experience the flash of inspiration that brings the vision into crystal-clear focus. The exact bits of information relevant to this process and the sequence of steps that result in the flash of inspiration are not apparent to the individual during this process, and they need not be. It is in many ways a magical process, like a bolt of lightning hitting the ground.

Once the flash of inspiration has occurred and the firm's innovation is in place, it is important to retrace the path of the lightning and to carefully inventory the steps that were involved. The firm must then exclude the steps that are not important to the ongoing implementation of the vision, even if they were instrumental in the process of discovery. The firm must arrange the remaining steps in an efficient, logical sequence. Because the path of trial-and-error is rarely the shortest distance between beginning and end product, the original trial-and-error path should not be formalized into routine practices. Failure to straighten out the path will result in costly inefficiency that will be built into all future practices.

A scientific laboratory that analyzed soil for traces of uranium, had a proprietary process for testing soil samples that was reliable and cost less than competing techniques. The firm achieved early success because of its innovative technique but, after about two years of production, had trouble increasing the capacity of the process. The firm charged $20.00 to analyze a soil sample, but the cost was $16.00.

My objective was to increase the capacity of the process. Prevailing sentiment was that the lab needed to double the size of the machines being used. Closer inspection, however, revealed that capacity could be increased by streamlining the workflow. The firm was still using a process very similar to the one they used to validate the original theory. It was a labor-intensive process that required the judgment of experienced staff to make certain that the process was proceeding as intended. With highly experienced staff involved, no procedures were written down because everyone knew the process inside and out. The temperature of the heating oven, duration of the plating process, and handling methods to prevent contamination all utilized the expertise of the staff.

Many of the less sophisticated steps also remained unchanged. Each soil sample was unpacked near the loading dock, carried to the front of the office for logging into the record book, and carried back to the rear of the lab for sifting and processing. The analysis results recorded in the front office were sent back to the customer via the loading dock. This too was much the same flow of activity used when the process was developed. However, the process then had used 25 samples, whereas the weekly volume now had become 500.

The experienced staff were unhappy because the thrill of discovery was over, but they were tied to a process that was making money, and they needed the money to support other research. They thought that if they doubled the size of their operation they could afford to hire and train new people to help them out.

Rather than simply buying bigger machines, I asked the staff to write down everything that they did to process the samples. This included, for example, all the preferred temperature settings and any indicators that the preferred settings might not be appropriate for a particular sample. This was not a pleasant process because it seemed like a very clerical one to these experts. They felt that all the education and expertise they used to judge the correct temperature setting could not possibly be distilled to a few simple steps or guidelines. Nor were they happy that someone who was not part of the early development was suggesting changes; an outsider could not possibly understand all the fine points of the process.

I persisted, they complied, and together we eventually identified several bottlenecks that kept capacity low. We streamlined the process by relocating the existing machines to fit the physical flow of the samples through the lab from the loading dock to the office where the results were recorded. We also found that less judgment was required for the temperature setting if they did a more thorough job of sifting the sample before it was heated. We got rid of several superfluous steps, and the costs were ultimately reduced from $16.00 to about $3.00 per sample. In addition, reliability and consistency increased because of the standardized procedures. Staff members felt more satisfied because they were released from jobs that had become routine and could focus their attention on more interesting issues.

It is a very different thing to separate the crucial from the superfluous steps and formalize production activities than to discover the technique in the first place. Discovery is creative, but the subsequent system should be more practical. Both approaches have their places. Unfortunately, the person who originally developed the soil sampling technique did not go back and systematize the process. In the early days, everyone was amazed that the process worked at all, and they felt a legitimate sense of accomplishment that their journey of innovation had ended successfully. The company had proceeded for a number of years dutifully following what they believed to be an innovative but inherently expensive and highly customized process.

How to Resolve the Problem

Foundation building is the natural next step after breakthrough innovation. To require some restructuring does not imply that the historical practices have been wrong or inappropriate.

The leader should set aggressive priorities to make the product or concept as practical, efficient, and clearly understood as possible. In some extreme cases, you may have to promote or transfer staff to encourage them to codify practices; people are more willing to share such knowledge as a way to leave a personal legacy. The priorities associated with this process denote the beginning of the Restructuring mode.

Chapter 5

Shifting into Second Gear

Chapter 5

Shifting into Second Gear

If you make a strategic mistake as the leader of a new venture, odds are you will make it right here, during the Foundation Building phase and the Restructuring mode.

You will feel pressures demanding action and change, but the pressures will be internal rather than external. Compared to the past, your instincts for how to interpret the signals indicating a need for change and for how to respond are likely to lead you astray.

If you get this phase right, you dramatically increase your chance of survival. Also, remember that this is just a phase, not a permanent affliction. It will come to an end. Do it well and you will come out on the other side to a situation that is likely to be more pleasing and comfortable.

Keep your wits about you. Realize that the purpose of this phase is to make your concept more objective, its processes more transparent, and, importantly, its use more widely accepted. This is the time to remind yourself that the key to survival lies in wisdom, choice, and action. Take a step back and try to see what the real impediments to growth and success are, just as Carl has done.

Carl Shifts into Second Gear

Carl's Model 3000 was now on the market. Yet while sales were increasing rapidly, it put a strain on operations.

Carl was sure they were just beginning to tap the market's potential. MaxCo was a major customer and had bought twelve Model 3000 units. FlashCo, a rival of MaxCo, had purchased seven units but required modifications for its units. These customized changes made it less imperative that FlashCo change its existing practices. Carl had obliged and, in fact, was pleased to do so because it enabled his company to satisfy a prominent customer. With these major customers and about two dozen others, the company was providing each customer the basic Model 3000 with many specialty features. While the Model 3000 began with certain standard features, Carl and the customer jointly designed each unit, and no two were alike.

As a result of all the special modifications, production and customer service were quickly becoming a nightmare. Carl realized they were going at 7,000 rpm in first gear. These were normal problems that come with growth that the company had to address. They needed to shift gears.

"I'm not going to step in this time," Carl thought to himself as he listened to his production manager, Alan, describe a production bottleneck. "The production team complains of being overworked," said Alan. "They are working late nights and weekends, and they are making too many mistakes," Alan asserted. "Everyone seems busy, but I don't even know what some of them are doing. To make matters worse, everyone seems to resent that I was made supervisor," he lamented. "Every time I ask them to do something, they ask, 'Does Carl agree with this?' or 'Is this the way Carl wants it done?' "

This time, Carl resisted stepping personally into the production room to troubleshoot, even though the immediate problem would be solved more quickly. Previously, Carl had intervened to solve problems, but he soon found that by doing so he was undermining the people he had assigned to take responsibility for solving problems.

A key difference this time was that he had delegated responsibility sooner. In the past, problems were detected at or just before a crisis point and therefore represented significant business risks, which absolutely required that Carl intervene. The problems coming up now, however, were not urgent, and so they had the time to work toward a permanent solution.

"Alan, let's talk about this in the weekly operating committee meeting," said Carl.

Carl had formed an operating committee consisting of the heads of the production, accounting, sales, and design departments. Although the whole company had only 18 people and it was tough to exclude some of them, Carl wanted a small key group to resolve internal coordination problems, advise him on policy issues, and communicate back to the rest of the employees. At first the committee meetings were used to exchange information while Carl still made most decisions. As time went on, the committee made more decisions.

After discussing the production bottleneck at length, Alan left the operating committee meeting with some ideas of how to approach the problem. He would meet with each production staff member to review what they did and what it accomplished, then solicit their suggestions for how to improve the process. In addition, they would involve the sales department to determine if the number of different versions of the Model 3000 could be reduced.

But to Carl, this was a dull life. The number of meetings seemed endless, and soliciting ideas held no excitement for him. He realized, however, that if improvements were to be made, he would have to endorse them and give personal attention to the effort. He recognized the impact of his personal priorities and that people were looking to him for guidance.

Carl could see progress in these efforts. He asked everyone to keep track of all the steps they were taking to accomplish certain tasks, the amount of time each step took, and any costs involved. He also created a business plan and mission statement and posted the mission statement in the employee lunchroom. Both were reviewed and updated by the operating committee and the rest of the company every six months. The objective of all these measures was to make activities and decisions more visible and involve more people in making decisions, and it seemed to be working.

The Foundation Building Phase

The Foundation Building phase is the time for a quiet internal revolution. Disassemble the priorities, practices, and structures that were successful in the past, and put new ones in place. You should be entering this phase by the time you have 10 people involved in decision making. It should be in full swing by about 20. The class of customer you serve won't change much; however, you should be surveying the scene for the most attractive market segment to target first in a direct and focused way.

Key Business Objectives

The key business objectives are to identify and simplify the essential elements of your product, to streamline production, and to formalize the business structure. During the Innovating mode, your product and organization developed in an ad-hoc manner. Now that both are more established, streamlining them will allow you to work more efficiently. Consider this adaptation from an 1822 essay by Charles Lamb.

———————

Centuries ago the great culinary delicacy of roast pig was accidentally discovered in a small village. One afternoon, a fierce fire burned down all the buildings in one part of the village. As the village people picked through the debris to salvage what they could, they discovered a pig that had been trapped in one of the huts. The discovery took place about dinnertime, and they decided to eat the pig. To their surprise, it was cooked perfectly and tasted quite good. It provided a feast for the evening, quickly became one of the most popular delicacies of the region, and was frequently created for special occasions. The only drawback was that every time they wanted roast pork, they had to burn down a hut.

———————

This is a similar situation to what occurs in many entrepreneurial ventures. Once they discover something, they feel quite gratified about their marvelous creation, but they keep repeating the same original process. Especially if the breakthrough is creative, an informal and intuitive decision process becomes part of the firm's culture and can create a legacy that negatively impacts the firm well into the future.

The founder of the organization and original staff are inherently insensitive to the need to simplify and restructure. Because they created the product and grew up with the organization, they have a thorough understanding of everything. However, if the product and organization remain as complex as they are after a typical successful Concept Development phase, you will run into some major roadblocks on your path to future growth. For example:

- New employees will require too much time to understand what is going on and how to be productive.
- New employees will fail to develop the expertise they need to make significant judgments because of their lack of personal experience with the product and its production techniques.

- Delegating tasks will not be effective.
- Decision making will have to remain more centralized than is appropriate for a larger organization.
- Selling your product and its benefits will take more time and expertise than new staff are likely to possess.
- Manufacturing practices suited to produce a small number of customized products will strain under higher volumes.

These weaknesses are significant, and if not addressed, their effects will hinder future business success.

Select the Most Influential Market Niche

During this phase, it is important for you to identify one or two of the most attractive market segments or niches that need what you offer. Even a small market, if handled successfully, can trigger sales in other larger segments.

There is a game popular in places where the winter snow and ice accumulate heavily on rooftops. By late winter, most buildings have huge clusters of icicles hanging from the edge of the roof halfway to the ground. The object of the game is to knock down as much ice as possible by throwing snowballs. If you make a big enough snowball and throw it hard enough, you can bring down huge clusters of ice. If your snowball is smaller or your throw not as hard, you bring down a small chunk of ice. However, with careful consideration of the how the various icicles connect to one another, even a small snowball can bring down large amounts of ice. Even among children, a practiced eye can identify an icicle that is a sort of linchpin for the rest. If that icicle is hit just right, it brings down a whole cascade of ice. Strategic thinking can overcome size and strength.

This is the same type of thinking that is needed during the Foundation Building phase. You need to pinpoint exactly where your company's product or service will have the most impact.

The Restructuring Mode of Operation

Typical themes of a restructuring organization are:
- Simplify.
- Fix it even if it isn't broken.
- Buy your shoes one size too big.
- Build for the future.

Begin to differentiate and systematize the tasks done by various people. Regroup the tasks in a way that makes sense for the future. The objective is to lay a foundation that will support the future growth of your organization and production of your product. This mode of operation is most appropriate for organizations that have from 10 to 25 members.

The organization and leader must focus for a period of time on the internal issues of establishing an infrastructure that is efficient and rational and that accommodates multiple decision makers. During this mode, you must begin to consider a broader range of issues; they will seem less dramatic and exciting than the issues of the previous phase. You must develop a more formal communication system and decision-making structure, keep records, develop accounting procedures, and establish control and monitoring systems.

Systemize Processes

In order to systematize the work already being done, you have to review the road you have taken so far. Look back to see where you have come from in the very early days to reach the present point. Appreciate that winding and circuitous path for what it was, a path of discovery. There are probably many parts of that path that are not necessary, and before the path becomes a well-worn highway, straighten out some of the curves. There is no longer a need to take the detours that were so important to the process of discovery.

Initiate Hierarchy

To create a hierarchy sounds like heresy to most entrepreneurs, but if you don't do it, your organization may crash and burn. If you do this now with the parts of your business that need it, you will not have to attempt it later when out-moded habits are harder to break.

Restructure the roles of people on the staff. In the Concept Development phase, people all worked together and were fairly equal in stature within the organization. During the first restructuring, you will need to promote a few people. They will begin to supervise and to take responsibility for the activities of others. This is a very difficult step in most ventures. In the past, everyone pulled together as part of one team. Some of those team members now have to rise above their peers and take leadership roles. It is difficult for people to rise above their peers, and it's difficult for the others to see someone else get ahead of them.

During the Concept Development phase, everyone had direct contact with the leader and could seek guidance one-on-one. Everyone could feel self-esteem, power, and influence by having direct access to the leader. Such access is now more limited, just by the fact that there are too many people within the organization for the entrepreneur to have direct contact with everyone.

Specialize

During restructuring is the time to introduce greater specialization of work for the members of your organization. Once an initial hierarchy is in place, rather than have everyone work on everything, have people begin to focus their efforts on a narrower set of activities. This, too, is difficult because in the past everyone has seen every part of the business, and they must now pull back and begin to specialize. Another reason that this transition can be difficult is that many of the people were hired for their generalist abilities rather than their specialist capabilities. One person doing many things was a great benefit early on because it enabled the organization to be so responsive.

Now the organization is more stable, yet the problems it faces have become more complex and require deeper expertise to be solved. You need people with specialized expertise to address issues like accounting, marketing, and production. In contrast to the Innovation phase in which there was essentially one decision maker, you now need multiple decision makers and formal decision structures to handle future growth of the business.

To many successful leaders of innovating organizations, this phase is unpleasant and, more importantly, boring; therefore, many entrepreneurs avoid it altogether or do not give it the emphasis it requires, in which case a decision-making vacuum is created. The leader tries to control the organization by using the informal controls and intuitive planning that were successful in the past. In this vacuum, some forms of structure and methods of control will begin to take shape. Unfortunately, without central coordination, they will not develop in a comprehensive and coordinated manner. Most likely, they will be ad hoc and cumbersome and will reflect the vested interests of their various architects.

A larger organization is more difficult to restructure. A rational and effective business infrastructure is a requirement for growth, and it will never be easier to build one than when you have between 10 and 25 people in your organization.

If you decide to grow but put off actively developing effective structures until later, restructuring will take much longer and be more difficult. With no formal structure in place, ad hoc and ineffective systems will develop in the void. These temporary internal structures are often fiercely protected later because they were the result of someone's personal effort to address a real problem. Dismantling these systems and then rebuilding takes longer than building them right early on. For example, it can be a daunting task to inventory everyone's job description and duties particularly if there are more than 25 people in the organization.

It is important for you as a successful entrepreneur to recognize the value of this first restructuring and to give it considerable focus and attention.

Most Effective Structure

A functionally segmented team is most effective for the Restructuring mode. In this structure, you reduce the span of activities for the generalist staff and assign clearer accountability, responsibility, and authority. Make decisions in roundtable discussions consisting of the heads of the functional groups. You will need to exclude some members of the organization from the central decision-making body in order to keep the number of attendees at a manageable level. The focus of the group is coordination of efforts and problem solving.

The first restructuring is a time for many meetings to exchange ideas about how to restructure effectively. Each person has direct knowledge

Evolution of Organizational Structure

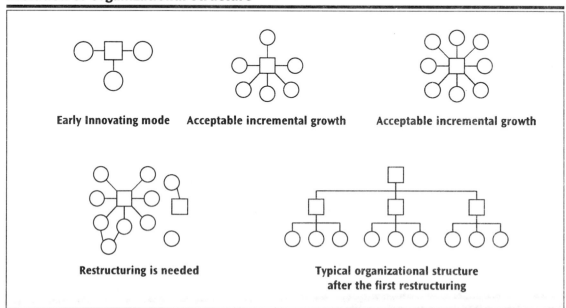

Early Innovating mode   Acceptable incremental growth   Acceptable incremental growth

Restructuring is needed   Typical organizational structure
                                  after the first restructuring

of what he or she has been doing. Take inventory of what everyone is doing, and group the tasks into general categories. Make sure the person best equipped to handle the tasks is responsible for doing them. Seek logical structures and separations for each person's responsibilities.

The Evolution of Organizational Structure diagrams show the sequence of structure from the early Innovation mode through the Restructuring mode as the organization grows. The squares represent decision makers, and the circles represent data gatherers.

This chart shows the typical progression within an organization during the initial phases of growth. The squares have true decision-making responsibilities. At first, each person has a direct reporting relationship with the leader. Eventually, the leader's ability to manage the rapidly growing functional areas is exceeded. Once there are more people or functions than can be managed by a single decision maker, you need to regroup by function and shift decision-making responsibilities.

Standardizing Your Product or Service

Pioneering customers who gave you the opportunity to understand their needs and to test your product enabled you to get where you are today. However, these customers, as early adopters, may not represent the bulk of the customers who could benefit from your product. Pioneering customers expect special features, and it is challenging and costly to meet all their needs.

Some of the features originally requested by these customers you may want to incorporate into the basic product for use by all your consumers. Now is the time to simplify your production processes by standardizing the product.

To standardize your product, go out and ask customers what they like about it. Find out what the common opinions are across your customer base. The tricky part of this exercise is to then identify the most basic product that will both reflect the essential elements of your innovation and serve the largest potential market. The goal is to define the simplest product with the fewest parts that provides the core benefits of your innovation.

Instead of adding features as you did during the Innovation mode, simplify your product to its essential elements in a form that can be produced in high volumes. If you have truly developed a breakthrough innovation, the market is likely to accept the standardized version and pay a premium for the product.

Rather than trying to satisfy all possible desires of all possible market segments, target a few market segments that you can quickly and successfully serve with a simplified version of your original product. If successful, they can lead to sales in other market segments.

Appreciate that you are able to sell the product widely, giving it the possibility of becoming the industry standard or the preferred brand or type. This process will take some time and should be done concurrently with your effort to build your business infrastructure.

Style of Management for Leader

The most naturally effective management style for the leader is collaborative engineer, a combination of the analytical and behavioral decision styles. Analytic leaders gather information before making decisions, and behavioral leaders tend to involve others in decision making. People with these styles promote effective communication among the leader, the staff, and customers. They are predictable managers and can patiently work through the personnel issues that are common during this phase. They also begin to break down the former tendency to defy everything external to the firm. This style combination is also effective for finding out what all the employees are doing, looking at it very logically, and deducing what should be done to structure it more efficiently.

Innovating was a hands-on mode. The leader was able to be directly involved in every aspect of the organization, including the product and the customers. The Restructuring mode is, by contrast, more of a hands-off mode. Lots of discussion and development are taking place, as well as shared decision making. When in this mode, you do not need to be involved in every decision. Instead, you need to set the correct broad organizational priorities.

This is a time of change, and change will be aided by creating a secure atmosphere for the staff. Each person will have to give up something. During this phase, they are often giving up their sources of power and prestige. They must be convinced that the change is not an indictment of their past efforts or a threat to their jobs. If the staff believe you do not care about them or their employment, they will resist changes in their jobs.

Talk to people. Listen to what they say. Members of an organization going through restructuring must sense that the leader and company do care about them. Mercedes Benz America is a good example of how to handle this well. They guarantee that anyone who eliminates their own job through improving techniques or restructuring is guaranteed employment.

Also, identify skills staff will need to become more specialized, and make sure that they get the training they need. It will benefit the company as well as the individual.

Expect Some Discomfort

The first restructuring is one of the most difficult transitions the entrepreneurial leader will have to make. A leader must move from being a decisive visionary to a collaborative engineer. A leader comfortable and energized by the Innovating mode can feel bored, uninspired, and depleted during Restructuring modes. Moreover, the method most passionately endorsed in the first mode cause grief in the second. The chart below indicates some of the contrasts between the Concept Development and Foundation Building phases.

The CEO's discomfort with the new mode of operation should not influence his or her view of its importance.

Shift in Priorities

Priorities During Concept Development	Priorities During Foundation Building
Creating bold new ideas and product.	Simplifying existing ideas and products.
Following intuition and defying conventional wisdom.	Reviewing market data and seeking the views of others.
Customizing for each customer; adding special features.	Paring down to the essential procedures and products.
Hiring generalists with ability to handle multiple tasks.	Hiring specialists with accountability and competence in specific areas.

Control During Restructuring

Although all methods of control are important in this mode, the most influential are organizational hierarchy and formal rules and strategies. A set of reporting relationships must be established and respected, especially by the leader. In the Innovating mode, everyone reported to the leader. During the Restructuring mode, other reporting relationships are needed. Formal rules and guidelines for performance, while they may seem legalistic, allow members of the organization to begin to make decisions more autonomously. This is part of managing the ebb of leadership allelopathy, the effect of the central figure minimizing the growth of those around them.

Additional formal methods of control that begin during this phase are personnel evaluation systems, company philosophies, and mission statements. As formal plans are kept, several people can begin to make plans more independently. Most of this effort is largely in preparation for greater emphasis in future modes of growth. These methods become operational but only at a low level during this phase.

Profile of Control Methods

Phase of Business Development	Concept Development	Foundation Building
Mode of Operation	Innovating	Restructuring
Important Controls	Supervision, vision	Broad range of controls
Controls	**Relative Weight**	**Relative Weight**
Direct personal interaction and supervision	60	20
Business vision	25	10
Cultural priorities	5	10
Organizational hierarchy	0	20
Formal rules and strategies	0	20
Expertise of individual members	10	10
Formal evaluation and feedback	0	10
Total weight	100%	100%

Control of the organization in this mode is broad, a sharp contrast to effective control of an innovating organization. Control during restructuring still depends on the personal influence of the leader, however.

It is important for the leader, who had little need for formal intermediate controls in the first phase, to come out and say, "These controls are important." This endorsement will have a far-reaching impact on all in the organization. If the leader is seen to demean the various controls, they may exist but they will have little impact. This is a tough balancing act, to stay involved enough to guide the fledgling controls and endorse their use while staying out of the picture enough to avoid undermining those administering the appropriate controls.

The Foundation Building Phase Summary illuminates the key features of the Foundation Building phase and the Restructuring mode of operation.

Foundation Building Phase Summary

Phase of Business Development	Foundation Building
Critical Objectives	• An efficient business infrastructure capable of supporting future growth. • A target market segment for expansion.
Appropriate Mode of Operation	Restructuring
Typical Themes	• Simplify. • Fix it even if it isn't broken. • Buy your shoes one size too big. • Build for the future.
Most Effective Organizational Structure	Functionally-segmented team. Close-knit and collaborative team with some individual members responsible for broad functional areas.
Cultural Priorities	• Proactively seeking opinions. • Objective research and fact finding. • Open discussion. • Codification of formerly intuitive practices. • Meetings to exchange information and form consensus.
Important Controls	• A broad range of controls. • Personal interaction with the leader. • Organizational hierarchy. • Formal rules and strategies.
Naturally Most Effective Management Style for the Leader	Collaborative engineer. Analytic with behavioral as a backup.
Prerequisites	• Sufficient business momentum to sustain a transitional period of restructuring. • Valid product and business concepts that are suitable for codification. • A suitable target for future growth.

Signs of Success

It is time to end the first Restructuring phase when work processes are structured and formalized, an efficient business infrastructure is in place, and a pivotal target market has been identified. A good indication that work processes are well codified is when new employees can step in to a job and be productive in a reasonably short period of time.

Limitations and Vulnerabilities

The primary limitation of the Restructuring mode is its internal rather than external focus. Because of this internal focus, the organization is using business momentum rather than building it. Restructuring cannot go on forever.

Undesirable Legacy

An undesirable legacy of restructuring is perpetual introspection. Decision-making is slow and ponderous. Every issue is reviewed from countless perspectives to make sure that no point of view is excluded. The issues, however, tend to be internal issues. External issues are not given the same attention. Deliberation takes precedence over action, and bold decisions rarely come forth.

You turned management's attention inward in order to structure your organization, but don't get stuck in perpetual introspection. It is time to proceed beyond the Restructuring mode as soon as you see the signs of success. It is time to refocus on external business opportunities.

Why It Is a Problem

Your organization is well run internally, but if you fail to pursue new market opportunities when they present themselves, you increase the chance of losing market presence.

How It Originated

This undesirable legacy originates from the internal focus and management style characteristic of a successful Foundation Building phase. The right management priorities for building a business foundation were internally focused and the collaborative engineer management style supports this. But once the infrastructure is built or the market environment changes and requires bolder action, the restructuring organization can be poorly equipped to succeed.

A Los Angeles-based manufacturer of mining equipment had brought in a new CEO to help it get its house in order during the Foundation Building phase. The leader was systematic and good with people, just the right combination for the restructuring. The CEO solved many of the problems that were apparent when he arrived. The firm now had a formal decision structure, and people were accountable for certain areas of decision making, with the authority to make and implement their decisions. Personnel evaluation policies and the training program were widely seen as fair, systematic, and appropriate. The firm began keeping records on the cost of everything to support informed decision making in the future.

However, it became apparent that the company was not moving aggressively enough to capture attractive segments of the market. The firm's products were available; the organization operated smoothly but, perhaps, too smoothly because selling was not a top leadership priority. Sales targets were set and later met. All targets were well researched, comfortable, and realistic. A far less methodical competitor appeared in their key market. This was not anticipated; nonetheless, the presence of this bold new competitor was clearly a barrier to their growth. After the company began loosing market share fast, a new leader was brought in to recast the priorities of the firm.

How to Resolve the Problem

There are ways you can bring the Foundation Building phase to a close before major hazards appear. One way is through proper timing. Ideally, you should focus attention on internal issues shortly after your innovative business concept has been validated in the market. When begun early enough, the momentum of the company's initial product success will carry the company through the restructuring period. You can also set specific objectives for the Restructuring mode so that once they are reached, everyone knows it is time to move on. For example, you might decide to develop all methods of control just to a workable level, with the idea that they will be refined in later phases.

Once restructuring is complete, your attention should become more external again. Realize that this change, like all the other changes discussed here, requires subtle alterations that may be difficult to recognize and achieve. But as long as you are prepared for change, you will be able to respond in ways that assure your business continued success.

A Fork in the Road

After restructuring, make a conscious choice as to which phase you will enter next. Your next move should accommodate the demands and opportunities the business environment presents. There are generally three broad types of business environments for a new venture after it has established its infrastructure, and each can be reached by one of the next modes of operation. While there is usually little that requires a firm to enter one environment and not another, you will find that some are more beneficial and easier than others for certain types of firms. Subsequent chapters will present each type in detail.

If you have access to a rapidly expanding market, take that direction. If this path is available to you, it is the one that gives you the greatest long-term advantage. Build a producing organization, a mode of operating appropriate for firms that have a large market for a single or small number of products.

The next most advantageous path is that of the Market Stabilization phase and a business environment that is complex and challenging but stable. The Planning mode is appropriate for firms operating in these environments.

The third most attractive path is toward the Niche Development phase. The business environment is complex, much like the Market Stabilization phase, but is also changing quickly, which makes planning futile. The Adapting mode is most appropriate because of its focus on adapting your company to serve the various segments of diverse markets. This may enable you to take advantage of higher profit margins for adapting to the customers' frequently changing demands.

Don't be tempted to select the target mode based primarily on which one is most comfortable. Instead, let your selection of the mode be driven by the opportunities available in the market. The selection process requires your strategic assessment of not only the market but also of your firm's capabilities.

Subsequent Restructuring Modes

Your organization will move through additional phases requiring the Restructuring mode as your company goes from one momentum-building mode to another. The nature of each restructuring between growth stages is very similar; the focus is on replacing existing power structures and work processes with practices that will support the new growth.

Differences do occur because practices that need to be developed are different. The new practices that should be in place for each growth mode noted in this book are the prerequisites of that growth phase.

Carl Restructures His Organization

Carl felt that the company was working smoothly internally, although it was somewhat over-built with a hint of bureaucracy.

"I hate filling out these purchase orders and time sheets," Carl complained to himself. He realized the value of such records in determining the real cost of what they did, but it still seemed like just so much paper work.

Carl's organization now had the decision-making system typical after an initial restructuring, as shown here.

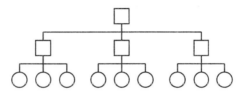

The heads of production, sales, and administration all reported to Carl.

One of the key business decisions Carl and his team made during this phase was to plan product strategy and find ways to eliminate some of the specialized features. They met with current and prospective customers, reviewed their immediate competition, and studied new market segments in order to evaluate the production implications of various versions of the Model 3000. They decided to offer essentially two different slimmed-down versions of the Model 3000, named Model 3001 and 3002, and to target FlashCo and others in its market segment.

The slimmed-down version incorporated the smallest number of extra features that would give access to the widest number of prospects in this market segment. These versions would incorporate the fundamental breakthrough innovation in a specific, tangible, and obvious way. The models would be simple to produce, even at high volumes, and relatively low in cost to the customer, considering the cost benefits of the breakthrough innovation. Sales would be fast and exposure to other market segments through this segment would be the broadest.

Chapter 6

Going for Market Share

The Rapid Market Expansion Phase

The Producing Mode of Operation

Most Effective Structure

Signs of Success

Limitations and Vulnerabilities

Undesirable Legacy

The Shift to Niche Development

The Shift to Market Stabilization

Chapter 6

Going for Market Share

Five, four, three, two, one, blast off. You have developed a breakthrough concept in the first phase. You constructed your launch pad and set your sights on the moon in the second phase. This is the time when you can ignite all rockets.

You are now in the Rapid Market Expansion phase and the Producing mode. During this phase, you will not have time to think deep thoughts or experiment with new paths. The course has been set and you have to make the most of the path you have selected. Focus and speed will be crucial to success in this phase and to your long-term success as well.

Carl Focuses on Production

"OK, everyone," said Carl in a loud voice to get the attention of everyone gathered in the warehouse. "We have a great innovation in the Model 3000 series, and we have spent some time making sure that we can produce it efficiently and manage our business while we do so. We have also identified some highly attractive market segments. These markets are very anxious for the basic features of the Model 3000. If we develop a good reputation in our target segment, it will carry over to other markets. Our goals for the next several months will be to sell as many of the standard Model 3000s as possible and to

improve the quality, consistency, and volume of our existing production capabilities."

Diane, the newly appointed head of sales, is ecstatic. She has a product. She has a story. She has a list of prospects. She is on the road.

Carl and Diane were a great team. They both liked to meet prospects and to make the sale, but they differed on two important strategic questions. The first was how much customization and servicing to do for prospective clients. The second was how long to make new sales the top business priority.

Customization came naturally to Carl. His discussions with prospects often became so-called blue-sky sessions during which he and the prospect would leap frog each other's ideas to create magnificent possibilities. Everywhere Carl looked, he saw opportunities for valuable new features. He kept mental notes of all the features that he and prospects had talked about. More importantly Carl, could easily see the technical possibilities of how customers' problems could be solved.

Carl also remembered with considerable angst, however, his attempt to expand the market with the dozens of versions of the Model 2000. Although readily accepted on the market, it was a nightmare to design, build, sell, and service all the different versions. Overall, the Model 2000 fell short of what they could have done in design, production, and sales because they had spread themselves too thin. They were, and still are, a small company. With the Model 2000, quality and reliability fell, as did customer satisfaction.

Diane saw the blue-sky discussions as a waste of time. To her, the faster they found that a prospect didn't want one of their current two versions of the Model 3000, the faster they could move on to the next prospect. It was a numbers game: the more prospects they met, the more they sold. To their good fortune, they had done their homework well because the slimmed-down Model 3000 was a hit with many customers. Ultimately, Carl deferred to Diane's judgment on this issue, and they avoided adding bells and whistles. Diane set sales targets, and her staff met them, or else.

The dominance of sales as the major management priority was something that Carl contemplated a great deal. It had been some time since the focus was innovation. Carl also knew they were a small company competing with large companies. As such they could not be competitive by giving top attention to everything. They had to be selective, and they had to select the right priorities.

While the team had done a good job of developing the current production system in the earlier phase, it was reaching capacity limits. Alan now had about a dozen people in his production department.

Adding new people increased capacity, but the system's capacity became a greater issue as time went on. To Alan, the systems issues were top priority.

"I believe we've had enough deliberation," interjected Diane during a discussion of production issues at the weekly operating committee meeting. "We have a good product. I do acknowledge that it is theoretically possible to make improvements, but they are not needed to meet our sales targets. Product quality is better than before, primarily because we are not trying to be all things to all people. Let's just get on with it."

Carl recognized that the nature of the weekly meetings had changed from coordinating and problem solving to simply assigning sales and production targets and pushing aside any barrier to meeting sales targets. It seemed to Carl that much was being swept under the rug, but he also knew they were operating in a privileged time, with a hot product, high margins, and little competition. "The priorities must be driven by the situation," Carl reflected. Alan had said they could produce 20 units a day, so Carl said, "Give me 25." Diane smiled.

With Diane's encouragement, Carl instructed Alan to make quick fixes to the current production system and to sound the alarms only when he felt production volumes or quality would drop. Quick fixes were more expensive long-term, but they were now gathering customers quickly at high profit margins. While they could afford the higher cost of quick fixes, they couldn't afford missing the chance to place product.

Alan was instructed to keep note of what production changes were needed but to hold off on major restructuring because they could not afford the down time. Carl stopped in to the production area from time to time, which he thoroughly enjoyed, to make a few improvements, just as he helped Diane's team refine its discussion of the feature of the Model 3000 and to help close sales.

This was a heady time. However, although rapid sales were exciting, to Carl, if it wasn't breaking new ground, it wasn't interesting. He longed for the old days.

The Rapid Market Expansion Phase

Once you've validated your concept, built some infrastructure to support additional growth, and identified which segment of the market will get your best snowball, now is time to act.

Your pioneering customers will give way to a wider market now that you have developed a stable product in a simplified version that lends itself to mass production. Now you can target one of the most attractive classes of buyer, the pragmatists.

Pragmatists adopt innovations later than pioneers but are more eager than conservatives to buy a new product and incorporate it into their lives and businesses. Their main concern is not new technology; instead, they do not want to miss a clear opportunity to make a fundamental improvement in the way they live or work.

Once they have made the choice to use your new product, they will turn their attention to realigning their activities around it. As long as the fundamental features of the product are stable, they can do without special features and are not sensitive to future changes in the product. They seek to get a head start on the masses that will follow.

Not all companies have access to a large segment of pragmatist buyers. Service companies often find that the number of these buyers is small relative to their conservatives or sophisticates. These service companies might stay in a Producing mode for less time than a company with a physical product that can be standardized.

Critical Business Objective

During the Concept Development phase you were extremely aware of your customers' lives and could identify what they needed. During the Foundation Building phase you inventoried all your customers' interactions with your product and company to identify the simplest, most easily mass-produced package of essential elements of the product. During the Rapid Market Expansion phase, you take this simplified product and put it into the hands of as many customers as possible. Your critical business objective is to sell more product immediately.

If there is a large market with no significant competition for your product, you should keep the product as simple as possible and avoid the temptation to enhance it. You were attentive to what customers wanted in the first two phases; you should now listen less. The priority is on getting new business and reducing the errors made in the basic production process.

This is the time to gain market share before possible competitors become fully aware of the business potential of your product or service. It is a time to build a solid revenue stream to support future efforts. Success in this phase depends upon the speed at which the product or service is put into the marketplace and how quickly production can serve demand. Success will attract competitors. When your initial production capabilities are straining and competitors are becoming active will be the time for your firm to move on to the next phase.

The Producing Mode of Operation

Typical themes of producing organizations are:

- Keep it simple.
- Do it.
- Don't fix it if it isn't broken.

Style of Management for Leader

While operating in the Producing mode, the style of management that is most effective is that of a decisive commander, based on the directive decision style. Their natural interest in specific objectives and quick action fits the needs of the Rapid Market Expansion phase of development.

Objectives are fairly clear and simple: to expand in the market, set objectives for the employees, and monitor the results. Compared to other modes of operation, there is just a one-way flow of information from the leader to the staff. This information usually consists of basic instructions about the tasks that must be accomplished.

The atmosphere of the firm at this point is a little like a classic old cartoon. The main character is driving an old jalopy with his partner at his side. A villain is chasing them, and they need to go faster in order to escape. He looks down at the speedometer and notices that the needle shows that the car has reached the top speed on the speedometer: 40 mph. In a stroke of brilliance that saves the day, he breaks the glass cover of the speedometer and writes 45, 50, and 55 on the speedometer. He then moves the needle to those higher numbers, making the car go faster, and they thereby escape the villain.

In the same way, the leader of a producing organization almost arbitrarily sets higher targets and commands the staff to achieve them.

An important point to remember is that the more of a breakthrough you create in the Concept Development phase, the greater your opportunity will be in the Rapid Market Expansion phase. Ironically though, as stated earlier, the more you have the management style to do well during concept development, the less likely you will have the management style to do well during a rapid market expansion.

Most Effective Structure

The organizational structure during this phase can be characterized as a platoon of implementors. Based on the general structure developed in the Foundation Building phase, members are added incrementally as the firm needs to grow.

Because objectives are fairly simple and stable over time, there is little need for an extensive middle management function. The organization is flat; there are few levels of hierarchy, and the senior people have many people reporting to them, as shown by the diagram (implementors are indicated as triangles).

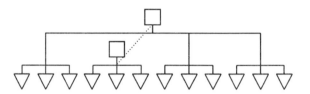

The leader formally supervises a relatively large number of staff, often over 10 people, and has informal influence over many others. These leaders will often go around their supervisors in order to influence activities in departments they do not formally head. This informal impact on the organization is illustrated by the dotted line in the diagram.

The Product – Minimal Customization

The product offered by a producing organization contains all the essential elements of the innovation but is not differentiated for various market segments or customers. Customization is kept to a minimum. When Henry Ford was in this mode, he said customers could have any color car they wanted as long as it was black. His focus was on getting the product out and expanding the number of his customers faster than anyone else. Even if there is no competition right now, if you are truly good, it is on its way.

Appropriate Business and Cultural Priorities

When you operate in a market that has a strong demand for your commodity or product, extensive planning is not a high priority because it will not have the payoff that it does in other situations. A high level of product customization will similarly have a low payoff. Sales expansion is the priority. The role of leadership in this phase is to encourage people to take action and to simply get the business.

The emphasis within the firm in a Producing mode is on setting and meeting specific objectives. These objectives may be sales targets, production levels, or service calls. One assumption implicit in this phase is that higher levels of market expansion are available simply for the asking. Interestingly, it is true that, if you have done a good job in the prior phases, higher levels of sales are readily available to a greater degree than many leaders assume. And if you aren't ready when the market is, you've lost the game.

By keeping the product simple, you can indeed increase volume and productivity as well as the quality of the product. High volume and repetitive cycles of work are a shakedown for your firm if you are using the first generation production systems developed during your Foundation Building phase. With high volumes, the inevitable weaknesses of the systems will be exposed.

When problems are exposed in a Producing mode, fix them quickly, even temporarily, and resume production. If it is possible to differentiate between a quick fix and a fundamental solution, favor the quick fix. Fundamental solutions should be designed into the systems during the next Foundation Building phase. Growth covers up a lot of mistakes. If you stop production for a long time to implement a fundamental solution, you will miss sales and the opportunity to get a larger share of the market. You will also miss the opportunity for a larger stature in the minds of potential buyers, which influences who they believe to be the premier supplier of your product.

One of the great ironies of new ventures is that the firms that have the greatest opportunity to focus their efforts on a narrow product line often are the least likely to do so. Firms that are first in producing a breakthrough innovation can offer a stripped-down version of the innovation and operate without fear of competition for a meaningful period of time.

Unfortunately, rather than taking advantage of this opportunity to focus on expanding market presence, they often place a high priority on adding bells and whistles, offering another new product, or developing the next breakthrough. They leave business to the firms that can copy the initial innovation and thereby avoid some of the challenge of their own Concept Development phase, starting right off in a Producing mode with an organization specialized for that purpose.

Apple Computer, for example, can produce innovative operating systems and software, but Microsoft, while not as innovative, can press their products into the market.

Controlling a Producing Organization

The most effective controls in the Producing mode are clear objectives, supervision by the leader, and activity evaluation and feedback. Direct supervision by the leader is more important during this mode than it was during the prior mode. In the Producing mode, the leader sets specific objectives for sales, production, and other areas and typically stays closely involved with the review process. Formal rules and hierarchy influence the behavior of all members of the organization, as clear lines of accountability and responsibility are emphasized. A successful producing organization also develops and uses formal evaluation systems to help its members understand how their performance compares with objectives. In this way, their activities can become self-correcting.

The Profile of Control Methods chart illustrates the relative importance (weight) of controlling the organization.

Profile of Control Methods

Phase of Business Development	Concept Development	Foundation Building	Rapid Market Expansion
Mode of Operation	Innovating	Restructuring	Producing
Important Controls	Supervision, vision	Broad range of controls	Supervision, performance evaluation, and feedback
Controls	**Relative Weight**	**Relative Weight**	**Relative Weight**
Direct personal interaction and supervision	60	20	30
Business vision	25	10	5
Cultural priorities	5	10	10
Organizational hierarchy	0	20	15
Formal rules and strategies	0	20	15
Expertise of individual members	10	10	5
Formal evaluation and feedback	0	10	20
Total weight	100%	100%	100%

The important controls during this phase are procedural. Interestingly, business vision is less important in controlling the organization than it was in the past.

The Rapid Market Expansion Phase Summary chart highlights the key features of the Rapid Market Expansion phase and the Producing mode of operation.

Rapid Market Expansion Phase Summary

Phase of Business Development	Rapid Market Expansion
Critical Objective	Expanding market presence, faster than anyone else.
Appropriate Mode of Operation	Producing
Typical Themes	• Keep it simple. • Do it. • Don't fix it if it isn't broken.
Most Effective Organizational Structure	Platoon of implementors. Information and task-oriented objectives flow from leader to others for implementation.
Cultural Priorities	• Focus. • Setting specific task-oriented objectives. • Quick fixes and tactical moves. • Following instructions.
Important Controls	• Direct and individualistic controls. • Personal interaction and supervision. • Performance evaluation and feedback.
Naturally Most Effective Management Style for the Leader	Decisive commander. Directive decision style.
Prerequisites	• Viable business concept. • Efficient initial business infrastructure. • Market demand that is stable enough that simple task instructions give members sufficient guidance. • Protection from competitors, such as technological, financial, and market access barriers.

Signs of Success

The key indicator that it's time to move on to the next phase is when competitors grab market share you reasonably might have gotten and seriously challenge your dominance. If you really have a good idea, you can be sure competitors will be attracted to your high profits, and their presence will make your business more complicated and volatile. Consequently, the simplistic strategies of the Rapid Market Expansion phase become insufficient.

Limitations and Vulnerabilities

The opportunity to sell a simple product to a vast market will not last forever. Competitors will ultimately be attracted to your success. The accumulation of quick fixes will also need to be reworked at a more fundamental level.

Undesirable Legacy

During the Rapid Market Expansion phase, the priority of the firm has been to expand market presence. Most other issues, such as refining internal capabilities, upgrading the abilities of the staff, or introducing an additional product, have been pushed aside. Unfortunately, the leadership of the firm becomes convinced that the good fortune will last forever. When competitors enter the market with a more refined product offered at a lower cost, the management is unaware of or underestimates the fundamental changes in the marketplace. The leaders fail to see that the situation has become more complex and unpredictable, and they race forward, as before, like lemmings into the sea.

Why It Is a Problem

Market gains are vulnerable to competition if there is no real plan for protecting them in the face of market saturation or powerful competition.

How It Originated

This undesirable legacy results from the narrow production focus of organizations successful in rapid market expansion. Their action orientation produces real benefits, but producing organizations tend to have poorly developed practices for scanning the horizon for trouble. They intend to keep running in the same direction, assuming the future will be as accommodating as the past.

An Atlanta-based manufacturer of athletic equipment had aggressively pursued market share. The firm had built an effective business and production infrastructure. The leader set concrete objectives for sales in each region of the country and personally reviewed the quarterly results to determine which had been successful. When problems developed with the new production system, she quickly assigned one of their best technical people to handle the problem and report to her when it was resolved. When staff problems arose, she moved those people involved with the problem to different production jobs.

She tended to view people as trainable and malleable and believed they could adapt to various technical situations. Unfortunately, the technical problems the firm was experiencing were actually symptoms of more fundamental problems that could not be addressed by a quick fix or by moving staff to other jobs.

Also, the leader focused her planning on sales targets and production levels. While useful, these statistics did not reveal changes going on in the market. Competing firms had entered key market segments and were taking market share. Thus, while her sales were increasing, competitors' sales were increasing faster.

Her competitors had entered the markets later and had learned from her firm. They had even better production techniques because of those lessons and were now able to expand more quickly with lower costs. She had misread the development of the market and was now unprepared for the situation she faced. Growth became much more difficult.

How to Resolve the Problem

The key is to understand that if you have a wide-open, attractive market with few competitors, the condition will not last long. Competitors will be attracted to your success and can benefit from the path you blazed. Aggressively pursue expanding markets that present themselves, but be prepared to reprioritize your efforts when the situation changes.

Of course, to de-emphasize the expansion of your market too soon is to give up market share, perhaps permanently. To make the shift too late puts you at a disadvantage because competitors have already defined the basis on which they will compete with you. As stated earlier, when your initial production capabilities are straining, and competitors are becoming active, it is time for you to move on to the next phase.

The Shift to Niche Development

Business opportunities for some firms that have experienced rapid market expansion, most notably software and some service companies, shift directly from the Rapid Market Expansion phase to the Niche Development phase. They must move quickly from being the only producer in their field to being one of many competitors trying to retain market share, provide customers with unique solutions to their problems, and increase or maintain their profit margins.

The Shift to Market Stabilization

Businesses that have a strong manufacturing or production component often find the next battlefield is on costs and functional efficiency. For these the shift is from rapid market expansion to market stabilization and the Planning mode of operation.

The transition from a producing organization to a planning organization is important because this is when the entrepreneur actually fully delegates decision making to others. During the first Restructuring mode, an alternative way of decision making was set up, and the business infrastructure was established. If the company has the opportunity to move to an expansion mode and stay there for some time, the entrepreneur typically has a great deal of control over the day-to-day activities. While the staff is gaining competence in their newly specialized areas during the expansion, the entrepreneur still supervises most of the activities of the firm.

As the company moves from a Producing into a Planning mode, the staff needs to work with greater focus and autonomy. The leader will need to establish rules, guidelines, and objectives in an unambiguous way that outlines the expectations for everyone's responsibilities without requiring the leader's close oversight. Establishing and using those guidelines moves the venture to the Planning mode.

Carl Faces the Competition

"Huh? Competition? How could anyone get here so quickly when it's taken us years?" thought Diane. Competitors were drawn to the profitability of the Model 3000. Diane, Carl, and Alan quickly studied the competing products to determine if the first battleground would be price or features or both. Time was of the essence.

Chapter 7

Fortifying Your Organization

The Market Stabilization Phase

The Planning Mode of Operation

Most Effective Structure

Signs of Success

Limitations and Vulnerabilities

Undesirable Legacy

Transitions

Chapter 7

Fortifying Your Organization

Not only do you have a great concept and product but you also have the world's attention. You pushed the frontiers of the market, and now it's time to step back from the frontier and fortify your position. What you built in the Foundation Building phase was the beginning of your fortifications; now is the time to complete the task of erecting the walls and roof and installing windows. Your survival will depend on how well you can plan and coordinate construction and how well all the pieces will fit together. You are now in the Market Stabilization phase and the Planning mode.

Carl Adjusts to the Changing Market

"Copycats! There's nothing original there."

"Just generic stuff. Cheap knockoffs."

"Those guys are nothing but cloners."

"Thieves ...."

Carl got the picture. It had taken special insight for him to create the idea, develop it, and begin to dominate the market. But any business with a healthy profit margin is bound to attract competition. Sure, he had blazed the trail, but that just made it easier for others to follow.

Carl still had some key advantages: nobody understood the concept the way his team did, he had the edge in quality, and he still owned the brand.

So the battleground was price. The new competitors were selling a product essentially the same as the Model 3000 for 25 percent less. They could get this advantage because they could take a fresh look at production techniques. Luckily, Carl had market share and money in the bank. He could therefore meet prices and build a new plant at the same time. Compared to their existing production capabilities, the new plant would have greater efficiency at higher volumes. They would finally be able to iron out some of the production problems that had bothered Alan for some time, and they could also offer more variations of the Model 3000.

Diane took the lead role over her sales team to focus efforts on keeping market share. Selling changed. It was tough for her and her team to shift their pitch from simply presenting the Model 3000 and taking orders to describing the features it had and the benefits it would provide to prospects as well as how their company compared to their competitors. The biggest hurdle was that the sales team had never gotten into the habit of asking the prospect about their needs and wants.

Carl now placed a high priority on operational efficiency. He developed a broad framework for how all the plans of various departments would be coordinated and combined. He was finally able to delegate complete authority to Diane, Alan, and others for their respective areas. By now, they were ready for it.

Formal planning was crucial. Their operations were going to be much more complex and the new plant very expensive to build; it needed to be built right. Planning included defining future business objectives, assessing progress, and dividing work among the various internal manufacturing functions and external subcontractors. Everything had to be planned out in advance to make sure that manufacturing produced what the sales team thought the customers wanted. The sales team had to make sure they knew, in fact, what customers did want. They hired people with experience in manufacturing, logistics, and management.

The weekly operations meetings changed yet again. Much less time was spent on sales and production targets and more on long-term planning. Problems were handled outside the weekly meeting, within the various departments. Any problem that did not clearly affect other groups was discussed within the functional group, not at a higher level. Each group had a set of specific responsibilities for current production and sales and for increasing capabilities. Carl had to be very careful to avoid giving direction without first confirming that the direction was consistent with the plans.

Diane and Alan were at risk. Both had grown with the company, but they lacked the specialized training and experience with other companies that would allow them to provide the depth needed in their respective functional areas. Carl realized that, while the company's past success was based on Alan and Diane's efforts, they were not adequately prepared to lead their groups in the future. Specialized skills were needed. Fortunately, business was unfolding as planned and, as members of the founding team, Alan's and Diane were richly rewarded for their contributions. Carl also realized that this, too, was a phase and that Alan's and Diane's expertise would be highly valued later on.

They decided that they would offer three standard variations, Models 3001, 3002, and 3003. These would serve the bulk of the demand in major market segments. With their gains in production efficiency, they could compete with any firm.

The Market Stabilization Phase

Once crucial tasks become stable and repetitive, they become programmable. Competition is based on a firm's operational efficiency, and this is where planning organizations excel. Manufacturing processes lend themselves to a Planning mode, but the technologies must also be rejuvenated periodically. Companies in the automobile industry present good examples of operating in this environment. Complex manufacturing processes are an inherent part of this business, yet technology continues to change the way the manufacturing process takes place. Computers, robots, and new inventory practices can increase the operational efficiency of the manufacturing processes. Periodically, these developments must be integrated with the existing practices. Without planning, inventories and costs surge out of control and losses appear.

Critical Business Objectives

You should develop greater efficiency in your firm's main functional areas, such as manufacturing, sales, and accounting. Your priorities in this phase are to specialize, refine the production techniques, and train the staff. Engineer these functions to ensure that quality is high and improving while costs are decreasing.

This is a very different mind-set than you were using before, especially in the Concept Development phase, but that's what it's going to take to beat the copycats at their own game. You'll need to hire the expertise that you may have avoided in your start-up days.

The Planning Mode of Operation

Typical themes of Planning organizations are:

- Measure twice, cut once.
- Let the data drive decisions.
- Select the right ruts.

Be careful when making plans and strategies. The decisions you make will influence your business for a long time to come. Double check the information on which you base decisions to make sure it is correct and right for the situation. After you have gathered high-quality information and analyzed it thoroughly, base your decisions on the outcome of the analysis. If proper analytical disciplines are used, they reflect defensible outcomes and reflect a disciplined way of making decisions. But be careful about the disciplines, procedures, and practices you select. Once selected, they will color your view of the world and how you operate in it. Any inappropriate biases will be built into your practices.

Style of Management for Leader

Improving the quality and lowering the average cost of each function require an engineering orientation, which is why the methodical engineer's analytic style is effective during this mode. Analytic individuals like to gather information and analyze it carefully before making decisions. This orientation allows you to identify all the variables that are involved in the product, serve the customers better, and fully understand the customers' needs and desires. Such an approach can result in a product that optimally meets those objectives.

Most Effective Structure

The most effective structure during the Planning mode is a hierarchy of functional groups. In this formal hierarchy, reporting relationships and responsibilities are clear and stable. Departments are often formed along the lines of whatever functions require the greatest degree of leverage, such as marketing, manufacturing, or accounting. The firm typically has limited specialized expertise in these areas, and market demands are stable.

By organizing around functional areas, the expertise of a small number of staff can be leveraged and used to train other staff. This structure is indicated in the diagram below.

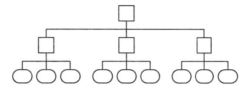

Decision making is also highly structured. Big decisions or projects are separated into smaller decisions, again usually along functional lines. The decisions about how to build a factory, for example, may be divided into components of transportation systems, the floor plan, and the utilities. Each component is addressed by a group of specialists with expertise in a related area, and their output comes together according to an integrated plan.

Don't entirely stifle that creative and innovative edge, however. You will need it later on.

Appropriate Management and Cultural Priorities

Remember that, during the earlier phases, new activities were developed using a trial-and-error method. Now many of these activities have become routine. Refine the methods and develop systems and processes to handle the complexities of the business that have become routine.

Training becomes important because you may need skills that are unique to your firm and you may be unable to hire staff with extensive relevant experience. It will help with growth during this phase if you hire people who have the needed expertise from bigger companies. By organizing your firm along commonly used functional lines, you have a better chance of finding people with previous experience relevant to your needs. This is not the time to create innovative structures or work practices. If you structure by functional area, it can help give you access to new staff already trained in the functional area, facilitate your ability to train the staff, and ensure high quality of output.

The efforts of each individual must fit with others' efforts within their department, and the same is true among departments. If they don't, a larger effort may be jeopardized. Clear rules, decision structures, and reporting relationships are some formal mechanisms of control that reinforce expected behavior. Interestingly, one of the hallmarks of this phase is that individuals and departments need to perform as expected; otherwise, the whole system doesn't work. Deviation from the norm is not valued in the organization's culture.

Controlling a Planning Organization

Organizational hierarchy and formal rules are important methods of controlling a planning organization. Formal rules are in the form of blueprints that indicate not only what pieces are needed but also how all the pieces should come together. There is relatively little emphasis given to monitoring and feedback on actual performance because of the assumption that success is planned into the blueprint. Of course, feedback is a significant part of a system, but in the Planning mode, most of the control is built into the plans and structure of the organization. The Market Stabilization column in the Profile of Control Methods chart shows the relative importance of the different control methods in a planning organization.

Important controls in a planning organization are procedural, emphasizing defined organizational structures and formal rules and strategies.

The Market Stabilization Phase Summary illuminates the key features of the Market Stabilization phase and the Planning mode of operation.

Profile of Control Methods

Phase of Business Development	Concept Development	Foundation Building	Rapid Market Expansion	Market Stabilization
Mode of Operation	Innovating	Restructuring	Producing	Planning
Important Controls	Supervision, vision	Broad range of controls	Supervision, performance evaluation and feedback	Formal rules and strategies, organizational hierarchy
Controls	Relative Weight	Relative Weight	Relative Weight	Relative Weight
Direct personal interaction and supervision	60	20	30	5
Business vision	25	10	5	5
Cultural priorities	5	10	10	15
Organizational hierarchy	0	20	15	25
Formal rules and strategies	0	20	15	30
Expertise of individual members	10	10	5	10
Formal evaluation and feedback	0	10	20	10
Total weight	100%	100%	100%	100%

Market Stabilization Phase Summary

Phase of Business Development	Market Stabilization
Critical Objectives	• Integration of your business with the rest of the business world. • Functional efficiency at high volumes. • Leveraging limited expertise. • Training large a number of staff.
Appropriate Mode of Operation	Planning
Typical Themes	• Measure twice, cut once. • Let the data drive decisions. • Select the right ruts.
Most Effective Organizational Structure	Hierarchy of functional groups. Groups are organized along functional lines, and the output of the groups is integrated according to predetermined plans and strategies.
Cultural Priorities	• Depth of analysis. • Use of defined strategies. • Predictable behavior and plans. • Functional specialization. • Consistency. • Hired expertise.
Important Controls	• Procedural controls. • Formal rules and strategies. • Organizational hierarchy.
Naturally Most Effective Management Style for the Leader	Methodical engineer. Analytic.
Prerequisites	• Viable business and product concepts. • Business processes structured in formal systems, plans, and rules. • Stable and predictable market for your products. • Staff with sufficient technical expertise in specialized areas.

Signs of Success

You'll know that you're succeeding in creating a Planning mode if you are able to compete successfully on price, deliver high volumes to large markets, and still maintain your edge in quality. This is no easy feat. Your success in this mode will show up in these primary ways.

Your systems such as accounting and production are refined enough to accommodate the stable complexities of doing business.

- Production costs are down.
- Your staff is trained to a level that produces a higher degree of individual autonomy.
- Price competition is fierce.
- The higher margins available in niche markets become more attractive.
- The grueling competition of the Market Stabilization phase may make you long for the excitement of the early days.

Limitations and Vulnerabilities

The primary limitations of this mode of operation are its lack of flexibility and resistance to new ideas. There had to be an explicit plan and concerted effort to get the departments to work together. But these plans can become quite complicated to develop and implement, and once they are in place, it is natural to resist going through this process again. New ideas that have not been tested or proven over time are given little credibility; thus, important changes taking place in the firm's environment may not be dealt with quickly enough.

Undesirable Legacy

The undesirable legacy of the Planning mode of operation appears as slowness and rigidity in the marketplace, resistance to change, and lack of advancement of junior members of the organization. It typically occurs when the business situation requires more flexible organizations able to adapt to new practices and opportunities for growth. Internally, the staff feel frustration from knowing they can offer more than they are providing in terms of judgment, and they feel constrained by the rigid power structure. Hierarchy, rules, and policies inhibit breadth of thinking and activity that would allow the firm to be more responsive and flexible. Because the changes to the power structure required to address these problems is threatening to those in power, the status quo is protected.

Why It Is a Problem

If the market becomes too varied and volatile for effective centralized planning, decisions will be too slow in coming and be poorly suited to the various market segments when they do come. Market opportunities will be grabbed by competitors that are more agile and responsive to market demands.

How It Originated

This undesirable legacy occurs when a planning organization tries to maintain a once-successful structure after it has outlived its usefulness. The systems, procedures, and policies established to handle the complex, but stable, activities of the firm are mutually supporting, but they are rendered out-of-date by a fundamental change in the market.

The success of planning organizations is based in hierarchies, detailed planning, and rules as methods to control the contribution of its members. However, as with the strengths of all other phases, these strategies can cause problems if used inappropriately. Leveraging the expertise of experienced staff is often done by having them lead functional groups.

Once the staff has been trained, however, the senior staff are often reluctant to allow newer staff members to use their individual initiative. In this way, the planning organization's hierarchy can serve to limit the advancement and initiative of the staff. Long cycles of analysis and planning slow down action and growth.

A Michigan-based manufacturer of trailer hitches depended on operational efficiency for its business success. Virtually all of its business was with the major car manufacturers that placed orders well ahead of required delivery. It had engineered its production techniques and clearly identified all the steps required of each worker. Decision making was formal and production procedures were highly developed. Each person played a well-defined role in the process, and the contribution of all workers came together according to an established plan and schedule. The firm was successful in reducing costs and meeting the needs it had anticipated in advance.

Then the company decided to sell hitches through the national chains of muffler shops. The muffler shops were anxious to add the sales and installation of hitches to their list of services. Sales were brisk and profitable. But muffler shops did not want to stock large numbers of hitches, and they could not accurately predict how many they would need well in advance of delivery. In addition, the variety of hitches required was great, and each muffler chain wanted the hitch assemblies to be modified to fit in with their own shop practices.

The manufacturer's management did not quickly understand the full impact of these diverse requirements. Of course they would try to accommodate the new requests, but they viewed these special requirements as exceptions to their existing practices rather than as an indication that they should contemplate deeper and more permanent changes.

The manufacturer's sales team serving the muffler shops complained that the production department was not being responsive. The sales team was concerned because one of the top muffler chains was seriously considering another supplier.

The production department countered that they were doing all they could, that the production runs did not allow any more variation. Revamping the current practices would require the attention of the most senior production people who were already busy managing the production staff. There was not much that could be done.

Ultimately, sales to the muffler chains stopped growing and began to decline. The production group saw this as evidence that the muffler shop business was simply a flash in the pan and, therefore, didn't justify any fundamental change. The sales team believe they gave away the business. Other hitch manufacturers were more responsive and developed highly profitable businesses serving the muffler shops.

How to Resolve the Problem

The first step to getting out of an obsolete rut is to recognize that you are in one. Define which aspects of your business need to become more adaptable. Certain core portions would remain stable, but others can be segmented away from the regular production cycle to accommodate the various demands of different market segments. Internal processes will need to be realigned away from the functional distinctions and toward the different market segments. This new alignment is characteristic of the Adapting mode.

Transitions

After a successful stint in the Market Stabilization phase, you will be ready for a transition. Two types of transitions are common.

When there is a fundamental change in the nature of the market that requires you to be more adaptable and flexible, your business is entering the Niche Development phase. The appropriate response is to create an Adapting mode of operation. This transition is difficult because it requires shifting from control centrally organized by product or function to control organized by customer or client segment.

The second type of transition is to a new and different stable market. You will still need to operate in a Planning mode, but the difference is that the stable practices need to be different. This transition is less difficult because the power structure does not require dramatic realignment.

Transitioning to the Niche Development Phase and the Adapting Mode

Tough price competition typical of the Market Stabilization phase may cause business leaders to seek out the higher profit margins available in niche markets. An industry-level example of this transition is the move of the U.S. semi-conductor industry away from the commodity-like memory chips to the higher margin of processor chips. Obviously this type of change is not a casual decision.

This transition requires a complete realignment of the power structure of the firm. In the Planning mode, the leaders of functional groups tended to dominate, and sales and customer service were support functions. In the Adapting mode, individuals responsible for client or customer service and satisfaction gain relatively more power. This shift is not easy because people do not give up power easily.

Although establishing the context for these changes is the role of the leader, the actual change that takes place between the Planning and Adapting modes is most difficult for the mid-level staff. The role of the leader is simply to set the broad priorities and to make sure that the power structures are dissolved and replaced with others that are more suitable. The intermediate structure between the Planning and Adapting modes is a matrix organization in which effective planning and coordination are in place but the leaders of the functional and customer service departments have fairly equal power.

Transitioning to a Rejuvenated Planning Mode

The transition to a new, rejuvenated Planning mode first requires a move to the Restructuring mode and then a return to a Planning mode that is better suited to the situation. Planning organizations are notorious for becoming rigid and completely inflexible. They often fail to update the inevitable small changes that are constantly taking place. Change occurs in all business situations, and for most planning organizations, small changes require little response. Over time, however, the accumulation of the numerous small changes results in the firm being out of sync with the requirements. Ultimately, a change is needed and the old system must be reviewed, purged of useless practices, and replaced with a new one. A new planning organization may be built, but it will be one with different stable practices.

Of these two alternatives, neither is inherently better than the other. A mistake that some leaders make is to assume that an Adapting mode is always the target mode. These days it is often assumed that everyone lives in a complex and rapidly changing environment; however, this is not true permanently. Customer demands often stabilize, and someone will think of a simple way to serve their needs in a more routine and cost effective way. This is one of the immutable trends in the world of business that must be accommodated: someone will always conceive of a way to systemize tasks that have become routine.

Carl Realizes the Need for Change

"We are running neck and neck with those hotshot competitors on price, and our margins have dropped. We are again at a crossroads," Carl thought.

Although Carl's company had achieved dominance in the industry and everything was working predictably, Carl sensed there was more business to be had. He began to snoop around and talk to all customer prospects, those who bought and those who didn't.

Chapter 8

Reaching for New Opportunities

The Niche Development Phase

The Adapting Mode of Operation

Most Effective Structure

Appropriate Management and Cultural Priorities

Signs of Success

Limitations and Vulnerabilities

Undesirable Legacy

Transitioning Out of the Adapting Mode

Moving Beyond Entrepreneurial Growth

Chapter 8

Reaching for New Opportunities

Get ready for hypergrowth. You developed your concept in the first phase and the business infrastructure in the second, you grabbed market share and got the world's attention in the third, and then you systematically fortified and expanded your market positions in the fourth. With these successes and the capabilities that launched them, you can now expand into a far wider range of markets with much higher profit margins and experience another phase of growth. This is the Niche Development phase and the Adapting mode.

If you didn't lose that creative, innovative spark but kept it alive, though subdued, through the Producing and Planning modes, then now is the time to bring it out when fresh ideas and products are needed. This is a tricky mode of operation because the organization will be highly sophisticated yet with a deceptively informal structure. And watch out for the stabilization and consolidation of market niches, which require part of your organization to develop a systematic way of operating.

Carl's New Opportunities

"Our Model 3000 is everywhere, but each customer has different needs," Carl pronounced at a company meeting. "We have 250

employees, and many of them have developed into experts in their fields. Our business infrastructure is solid, our core production disciplines are second to none, and our market is huge. But before our competitors mimic everything we do, let's be the first to take the next step and spray the market with dozens of versions of the Model 3000. We can charge higher prices because we are meeting more of our customers' needs, and that will make it more difficult for competitors to challenge us head-to-head."

Carl was stepping back into his element. Visualizing possibilities is what he liked best, but he had to hold himself back a bit. Rather than promoting fundamental revolutions in the industry, his mission was to listen to his customers and give them what they wanted, down to the smallest detail.

The company designated people from the sales, production, and design teams to form three groups. Each group had representatives of each function. Groups were asked to find out everything there was to know about certain segments of customers, particularly how customers were presently using the Model 3000. The teams sought to understand the entire context of activity in which the Model 3000 was used or could be used. Their goal was to make its use more efficient and effective for customers.

The big issues for the company were first to create the new teams to study the market segments and second to integrate these new market-oriented teams with the other internal functional groups that remained unchanged. The latter was most trying.

Amy, the head of the manufacturing department, was concerned because manufacturing was no longer experiencing rapid development and, therefore, garnering management attention. Amy resented what she saw as the rise of marketing to a higher stature than manufacturing. No longer was the marketing function simply to sell what Amy's department produced, but Amy was supposed to listen to the marketing teams regarding how to make the Model 3000 products better.

"These teams have some of the best people from my department. They know their stuff and their suggestions are rational and doable, but we are no longer in control of our own destiny," Amy complained to Carl.

The creation of the market-segment teams was reminiscent of the early days for Carl. Staff members who could engage in blue-sky discussion were most helpful. In fact, Chris, the highly conceptual designer selected to be on one of the teams, made an immense contribution because he could understand intuitively what was happening inside the customers' shops. Together with other team members, Chris' team specified customized products that were enthusiastically accepted by customers who once thought their needs were too unique to benefit from the Model 3000. Chris' team was able to design the customizations and work with manufacturing to make it happen efficiently. Effective product design and team collaboration came about with the help of computer systems and clever communication techniques such as special e-mail access so everyone could stay current with each team's progress and input.

Carl realized that he had to promote a new sensitivity to client demands. He wanted the company to build on the operational efficiency developed in the last phase and to emphasize listening to the customer. He encouraged even parts of the company that did not change structurally to think about the customer's situation and look for opportunities to provide solutions.

The nature of the operational meetings shifted again. They were now monthly meetings called strategy sessions. Less time was spent on the long-term planning of specific, measurable objectives. Those tasks were well taken care of by the business units and the functional departments that were now given much more discretion in how they developed and executed their plans.

The strategy sessions were more about targeting new business opportunities and trying to understand the subtleties of markets. In addition, personnel issues became important topics of discussion. This was not so much to solve individual issues, which was done in the teams, but to address how to hire, train, and motivate employees, as well as how to channel their energies and interests. More and more, staffing became the constraint that limited growth and the ability to implement business strategy.

The risk of fragmentation inherent in firms organized by market segment was reduced by the fact that the basic business disciplines were similar across the units. Also, the staff had, on average, a high level of expertise in all business matters, and internal communication was excellent. Trust within each team and among the different teams was high.

Carl and the heads of the departments set the broad direction for business growth and monitored results. The strategies used by the units to support the business direction were left up to the units as long as they did not violate the company's broad policies. To ensure compliance with the intangible aspects of policy and culture, Carl and others made it a habit to walk around the company every week. They talked to people, listened, exchanged views, and provided encouragement. Carl knew that every person in the company was making several decisions a day that had an impact on the business. In addition, most of the people in the company were closer to the customers than Carl and the management team were. The ideas, thoughts, and concerns of the front-line people were of vital importance.

The Niche Development Phase

The customers willing to pay more for special features might be able to be grouped into market segments, but the makeup and the demands of these segments change quickly. Responding effectively to this changing situation defies being reduced to formal plans and systems. Instead, you need to depend more on the flexibility of your people. You will need to guide them with a vision and trust them to implement that vision effectively for their market segment.

Critical Business Objectives

The most pressing issues during the Niche Development phase vary from market segment to market segment. For example, the tastes of your customers, the capabilities of your suppliers, and the activities of your competitors may change quickly and thus make it difficult to accurately predict how your efforts should be coordinated. In these situations when you may not be able to develop detailed plans, adaptability is essential and intuition is again needed. Therefore, the critical business objectives for you now are to listen and adapt.

The Adapting Mode of Operation

The typical themes of an adapting organization are:
- Create synergy from collaboration.
- Listen to the customer.
- Use cross-functional teams.

This mode of growth is well suited for situations that are complex and change more quickly than in earlier phases. Once your firm has restructured its functional areas to reduce costs and increase efficiency, the pendulum should swing away from operations toward the customer.

Your firm can adapt to the unique features and demands of individual market segments. It is time to dismantle some of the rigid functional departments and, instead, form them around opportunities presented by different market segments or niches. This structure, which is usually used for just a portion of a firm, will allow each team to produce goods that are valuable to specific market segments. To adapt the basic products or services to the particular needs of these market segments requires creativity, energy, and agility.

Style of Management for Leader

The naturally most effective style of management for the leader during the Adapting phase is as a collaborative visionary, which reflects the conceptual decision style with the behavioral style as the backup. These leaders readily create a vivid, broad image of the industry, the company, and its opportunities. They infuse the organization with a strong culture that helps guide the actions of its members.

Collaborative visionaries listen to others, seek consensus, and place a high value on interpersonal communications. They act as a clearinghouse for strategic information concerning the various units of the organization.

Adapting organizations place high value on corporate culture and philosophy to guide the independent decision making of the staff. They accommodate the intuition of their members. Compared to the other modes, it is less critical that the leader of an adapting organization match this profile because decision making in adapting organizations is decentralized, which reduces the day-to-day impact of the leader.

Most Effective Structure

Adapting organizations are a federation of teams. A market driven team is established to serve each segment of the market in a manner tailored to the needs and demands of that market. The teams typically cut across the functional areas, with marketing, production, sales, product design, and so forth, to bring all functions together to serve that market segment. This structure is indicated by the following diagram.

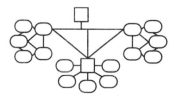

Formal structure and centralized planning are often not effective because each market-segment group must be able to respond to the peculiarities of its own market segment. This loose collection of groups should be united when possible by policies, shared technology, and a common overall business philosophy.

Appropriate Management and Cultural Priorities

The Adaptive mode requires you to place high priority on the ability of each market-oriented team to work across functional areas. This requires a strong positive culture and strong personnel practices. In addition, you must assure that independent decision makers within the team are supporting the broad vision of the company.

Controlling An Adapting Organization

Within the market-oriented teams, people do not have the benefit, nor the confinement, of direct supervision by the central leader or of rigid policies, guidelines, or rules to help them make decisions. During this phase, the firm depends on members of the organization to use their own initiative, judgment, and interpretation of the organization's broad objectives. Because the company-wide objectives cannot possibly be specific enough for every situation encountered, the firm's general philosophy and culture act as important guidelines for how people should act and behave. Common philosophies, group identity, and sense of being a part of an organization are very important methods of control for the firm as a whole. Also, if one group is not performing up to standards, its poor performance could hurt the firm's reputation.

The most important methods used to control the organization during this phase are the expertise of its members, formal personnel evaluation and feedback, the organization's culture, and its business vision. Adapting organizations rely on each member of the organization to make decisions that are in the best interest of the firm. A fair, positive, and supportive culture promotes this behavior. The culture should be reinforced with appropriate personnel policies, such as compensation packages, benefits, a bonus system, and career opportunities. Those you developed earlier really pay off now.

A common weakness of organizations moving from a Planning mode to an Adapting mode is an inadequate feedback and evaluation system. Although such systems are typically developed in the Market Stabilization phase and Planning mode, they were not a main form of control then so may need strengthening to be one of the main methods of control during this phase. Also, because formal feedback and evaluation systems appear rigid and seem to go against the flexible nature of an adapting

Profile of Control Methods

Phase of Business Development	Concept Development	Foundation Building	Rapid Market Expansion	Market Stabilization	Niche Development
Mode of Operation	Innovating	Restructuring	Producing	Planning	Adapting
Important Controls	Supervision, vision	Broad range of controls	Supervision, performance evaluation and feedback	Formal rules and strategies, organizational hierarchy	Vision, culture, members' expertise, performance evaluation
Controls	Relative Weight	Relative Weight	Relative Weight	Relative Weight	Relative Weight
Direct personal interaction and supervision	60	20	30	5	5
Business vision	25	10	5	5	20
Cultural priorities	5	10	10	15	20
Organizational hierarchy	0	20	15	25	5
Formal rules and strategies	0	20	15	30	10
Expertise of individual members	10	10	5	10	20
Formal evaluation and feedback	0	10	20	10	20
Total weight	100%	100%	100%	100%	100%

organization, they are often not given adequate attention. Yet they are a crucial mechanism to make the whole system work together to achieve positive results.

The Niche Development Phase Summary chart on the next page gives the main features of the Niche Development phase and the Adapting mode of operation.

Signs of Success

The Adapting phase comes to an end when multiple competitors offer a number of products similar to those you offer each market segment and when the differences between the products cease to be economically meaningful to the customer. Customers are no longer willing to pay a premium for the more customized goods, so the higher costs of having market segment teams force some firms to consolidate along functional lines again in order to lower the costs of production.

Niche Development Phase Summary

Phase of Business Development	Niche Development
Critical Objectives	• Response to the complex, changing needs of different market niches and segments. • Innovation driven by the articulated needs of the market.
Appropriate Mode of Operation	Adapting
Typical Themes	• Create synergy from collaboration. • Use cross-functional teams. • Listen to the customer.
Most Effective Organizational Structure	Federation of cross-functional teams. Teams are formed according to market segments to represent a wide range of functional specializations. An extensive information network envelopes the entire federation and supports numerous decision makers.
Cultural Priorities	• Adaptability. • Focus on customer input. • Pervasive informal communication. • Thorough knowledge of market segments. • Sense of urgency and shared destiny. • Flexible strategies.
Important Controls	• Abstract and individualistic. • Loyalty-inspiring vision. • Strong cultural priorities. • Expertise and judgment of individual members. • Activity feedback and evaluation.
Naturally Most Effective Management Style for the Leader	Collaborative visionary. Conceptual, with a strong element of behavioral.
Prerequisites	• Employees with a high level of expertise. • Stable and efficient business, information, and communication infrastructures. • Strong and effective formal feedback and evaluation systems.

Successful firms then move back to a Planning mode in order to lower costs, with a small segment of the firm operating in the Innovating mode dedicated to creation and development of a new breakthrough innovation and market niche. Thus, the cycle of development begins again. The next chapter will describe an overview of the complete cycle and how restarting applies to established companies.

Limitations and Vulnerabilities

An adapting organization is a high-cost structure. Maintaining the alliance of diverse units may become too costly compared to the overall benefits. The high-expertise teams that are organized to serve a segment of your marketplace may find it too difficult or time-consuming to learn about all the other parts of your organization in order to represent them appropriately. They may find that they derive little benefit from a connection with the larger organization. The teams can break away from your company and start their own. Your company can easily spin out of control.

Another risk is the potential for infighting between teams that have customer service as a top priority and teams with an operational priority. This is a risk whenever an organization has an adapting element coexisting with a planning element. The solution is to clarify objectives and emphasize how each plays an important role.

Another danger is that the CEO becomes out of touch with the day-to-day realities of the business. In an effort to expand the federation, he or she experiments with distractions, like buying unrelated businesses.

Undesirable Legacy

The undesirable legacy of the Adapting mode appears as a bewildering array of product variations that fail to be appreciated by a sizable market. Market-segment teams are working semi-autonomously to meet the needs of their segment of the market. Yet different teams are addressing essentially similar problems and coming up with solutions that are different only because they were developed by different teams. Although the customers may be satisfied with the solutions presented by the teams that served them, they may also have been just as satisfied with a solution developed by another team. The solutions are distinct, but there may be no meaningful difference that customers would be willing to pay for. The result is customization but at a higher cost for no reason.

Why It Is a Problem

This situation represents a duplication of efforts. Of course, not every customization will become a distinction without a difference, and the organization will need to determine how much true duplication it can tolerate in order to get customization that has a significant business impact.

How It Originated

This undesirable legacy is based in the semi-autonomous team structure of the adapting organization. The cross-functional teams can develop a tremendous variety of outcomes. As markets become more homogeneous and standardized, many of the differences are no longer meaningful.

Also, with a focus on developmental innovation, the market-segment teams tend to have a shorter-term focus and respond to market needs rather than to anticipate them. The company may devote time, money, and attention to customization and miss opportunities for breakthrough innovation by failing to see broad trends emerging across the market segments.

A New York-based money management firm tried hard to listen to its customers. It established three separate teams to work with large, medium, and small clients. The culture and philosophy of service for the company was strong and enabled each team to deliver service that could be identified with the organization as a whole. The reputation of the firm was strong.

As time progressed, their clients' businesses grew and changed. The classifications of large, medium, and small no longer related to differences in what each required. The needs of the market segments were converging and stabilizing. This gave the firm an opportunity to consolidate some activities performed by each team.

Unfortunately, the different teams responsible for the segments wanted to retain their relative autonomy and did not want to be consolidated. They pointed out differences in how each segment was being served and how each team had developed their own reports evaluating the investment performance of accounts. Each report was different in appearance, run by different people, and based on different software packages.

Because of the duplication of efforts, costs were high, but more importantly, the organization's segmentation prevented any one person from seeing trends developing across the segments.

The teams were so focused on satisfying current market needs that they had little time to think about their business as a whole. The staff did not have the vision to anticipate broad trends, and they were late to spot the really important trends affecting the whole industry. Because of this market myopia, a new firm consisting of just a few people successfully identified the emerging trend.

Although the markets served by both firms continued to grow, most of the growth went to the new firm.

How to Resolve the Problem

The solution is to look proactively for ways to consolidate activities that are common to all segments. Doing so will free up resources that can be used for new opportunities.

Transitioning Out of the Adapting Mode

An adapting organization is able to move into complex and volatile marketplaces because it is responsive. Over time, however, as the once changeable nature of the market segments becomes more predictable, the organization can identify ways of systematizing the uncertainties and complexities.

As the organization establishes its products within these new, marginal areas, there is a risk that the marketplace may become saturated with a variety of products and become too fragmented. If this happens, the market may change as the variety of services consolidate. Thus, there may be a movement back to a more predictable environment. If this is the case, the expensive customer-oriented structures will become too costly, forcing a restructuring of the firm along lower-cost functional lines. A shift to the Restructuring mode and ultimately a Planning mode would be appropriate.

Ready for a New Breakthrough

As Carl surveyed the facility his company had built, he realized that he had a state-of-the-art manufacturing facility and marketing and client service teams with deep knowledge of customer needs and the ability to respond to business opportunities. He also recognized that the Model 3000 technology had run it course. In addition, they had derived all the benefit possible from developing versions for niche markets. Amy grouped the 12 different customized versions that had developed over the recent phase and identified how they were starting to stabilize and converge. It would be possible, she believed, to simplify the product line and still meet the wide range of client demands.

Recently, demand had indeed converged, and there was less need for the market-segment groups to identify and serve the unique market niches. Carl decided to reduce the product line to four standard versions and cut prices to draw in the customers who would not otherwise buy.

He also realized that it was time to develop the Model 4000, the next breakthrough innovation. Chris' team had identified a significant problem for a customer and proposed a novel solution. Carl had assisted them on the effort and saw immediately the broader application for the technology. Quietly, Carl, Chris, and a few others rented a small warehouse to develop the concept. Carl and Chris were in their element.

Moving Beyond Entrepreneurial Growth

Ultimately, your organization may have elements of all modes of operation. Furthermore, each department and activity can have its own appropriate structures and priorities, with each one proceeding along its own developmental path through the phases of development.

As you continue to create new lines of business, each one should proceed along its own developmental path. Then it becomes less necessary for you as the leader to develop any one particular management style. The leader's role is then to identify what kind of emphasis should be placed on the newly developed business efforts to shepherd each unit through its own developmental process. Ultimately, different departments should be structured differently depending on the nature of the decisions and opportunities they deal with. For example, the accounting department may be structured differently from the marketing department, and the research department may be in a different phase than the manufacturing area. Thus, a firm may be primarily an adapting organization, but it may have distinct departments or units that are going through a Planning mode or even an Innovating mode.

Chapter 9

Know Your Location and Destination

Identify Your Situation

Know When to Shift Gears

Trajectory and Momentum

The Importance of Periodic Review

Different Businesses May Take Different Paths

Recognizing Inherent Weaknesses of Each Mode

Know Your Location and Destination

As the leader, you should continually be aware of which phase your organization is in, as well as anticipate the upcoming phase. By knowing the phase you're currently in, you can ensure that your organization is operating in the most effective mode for that phase. By having your sights set on the next phase early, you can begin proactively making the decisions and changes necessary to ensure a smooth transition to the next phase and its appropriate mode.

Identify Your Situation

The chart on the following page provides a way to quickly determine the optimal combinations of management style, organizational structure, and other factors for each phase.

Appropriate Modes of Operation in Each Business Phase

Phase of Business Development	I. Concept Development	II. Foundation Building	III. Rapid Market Expansion	IV. Market Stabilization	V. Niche Development
Appropriate Mode of Operation	Innovating	Restructuring	Producing	Planning	Adapting
Management Style for Leader	Decisive visionary	Collaborative engineer	Decisive commander	Methodical engineer	Collaborative visionary
Organizational Structure	Team of focused generalists	Functionally segmented team	Platoon of implementors	Hierarchy of functional groups	Federation of market-driven teams
Management and Cultural Priorities	Insight, new ideas, action, agility	Open discussion simplification, systemized work processes	Narrow focus on production and following instructions	Data-driven decisions, defined strategies, refinement, cost reduction, consistency	Informal communication, knowledge of market segment, flexible strategies, cross-functional teamwork, mass customization
Important Controls	Supervision, vision	Beyond range of control	Supervision, formal rules, feedback	Formal rules and strategies, organizational hierarchy	Vision, culture, members' expertise, performance evaluation
Class of Buyer	Pioneers	Same as prior mode	Pragmatists	Conservatives	Sophisticates
Product Strategy	Custom and innovative products developed for a small number of partner-like customers	Same as prior mode	Commoditized version of the innovation offered to customers willing to pay premium prices	Standard product line to a large number of price-conscious customers in stable market segments	Customized versions of the products to a small number of customers in various market niches

The road map introduced earlier can be developed further to describe the nature of each phase of development and key variables that make up each mode of operation. As shown in the Road Map below, each of the five modes of operation is associated with a specific type of business situation, management style, organizational structure, and typical class of buyer.

Road Map – Version 2

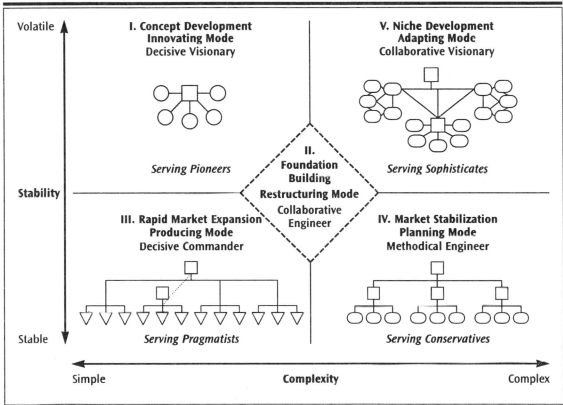

In the diagram, the squares represent decision-makers and the circles represent people who gather information. The squares with rounded corners are both data-gatherers and decision-makers, and the triangles are implementors. The Restructuring mode should be used when moving between any of the other modes. Moving from one market-oriented phase, those appearing at the corners of the diagram, to another is far less effective if attempted without formal restructuring.

The horizontal axis represents complexity and refers to the number or variety of key issues that must be considered when making decisions. Usually, the key issues relate to the business environment, your product and product development, or to the organization. The more complex the issue, the more it must be separated into smaller units and delegated to others. The less complex the issue, the more decision making can rest with individuals.

The vertical axis represents stability and refers to how predictable the issues are. The more volatile the issue, the less useful formal planning will be. When issues are less volatile, plans, systems, and machines can be made to handle them in an effective and efficient manner.

You can see from the diagram that the Concept Development phase and Niche Development phase generally present situations in which issues are volatile and unpredictable. Rapid Market Expansion and Market Stabilization phases, on the other hand, often present situations that are stable and predictable. The map also indicates that the Concept Development and Rapid Market Expansion phases generally involve situations with relatively few major issues that command the attention of leadership. In contrast, the Market Stabilization and Niche Development phases are often more complex in terms of the variety of issues leadership must deal with.

As you can see in the Road Map, the complexity and stability of your management situation changes for each phase of your organization's growth. To lead the organization effectively during each phase, you must understand the decision-making requirements of each type of situation.

Unpredictable, Simple Situations

Unpredictable situations that are relatively simple, those of the upper left-hand quadrant, call for quick and intuitive decision making by individuals immersed in the situation. This situation is similar to a crisis when a major issue rapidly emerges to the forefront and other issues fade into the background. An individual has to assess a lot of information not easily identified in advance and must respond quickly to the situation. These situations can usually be effectively handled by one person. This is characteristic of the Innovating mode.

Simple, Stable Situations

In situations that are simple and stable, those in the lower left quadrant of the chart, decisions are made in a fairly typical manner. It is obvious what should be done because the information required for the decision is simple and stable over time. Information can be evaluated and scrutinized by a number of people to identify the appropriate decision and predict the appropriate outcome. The standard, readily acknowledged decision or answer is probably most effective. This is true for the Producing mode.

Complex, Stable Situations

In situations that are complex and stable, those in the lower right quadrant of the chart, decisions are typically made by devoting effort to researching and analyzing the situation to identify the best way to proceed. Because the relevant information is relatively stable over time, once the analysis is done and done well, there is no need to rethink the analysis and decision. Any systems or plans developed as a result of this analysis are useful for managing the situation in the future, thus making such an investment worthwhile. The situation can be decided and the response programmed in advance. This is characteristic of the Planning mode.

Unpredictable, Complex Situations

For unpredictable situations that are more complex, those of the upper right quadrant of the chart, more than one decision maker should be involved. It is not possible on an ongoing basis for a single individual to adapt quickly enough in all the situations that must be addressed. To be most effective, a team should make intuitive decisions about one portion of the overall situation. For the leader to work through other people requires a more consensus-oriented decision-making process. This is true for the Adapting mode.

Road Map Keys

Based on the complexity and stability axes, the right half of the Road Map diagrams indicate phases of growth that depend more on the leader working through the organization to achieve success with an issue. The left half, on the other hand, indicates phases that depend relatively more on the leader's personal handling of an issue. The top half of the diagram indicates growth phases that depend most on individuals being thoroughly knowledgeable of the volatile issues. In contrast, the bottom half indicates phases that depend on operational efficiency for success.

Know When to Shift Gears

As you experience the transitions that your organization undergoes to operate in the mode best suited to a situation, expect some crises to occur. The development of a viable business organization is not smooth and linear. Ups and downs are part of successful growth.

Think of developing a successful business as being similar to driving a manual-transmission car. You use a combination of engine speed and a series of different gears to get to the top speed. When you start, you can gain speed simply by pressing on the accelerator to give the engine more fuel. This works great for while, but after a certain point, you can't go faster just by giving it more gas. You've got to let up a bit on the gas and, doing some fundamental changing in the mechanics of the car, you shift to a different gear. In order to shift gears, however, you must have enough momentum to keep you going when you let up on the accelerator. If you do not have enough momentum to get into the next gear, you drop back and give it another try.

This is similar to the ideal way to lead an organization through the various phases of growth. You achieve the maximum possible results with one mode of operating, and then you make some fundamental changes to allow you to continue growing. To make these changes, however, you need to have enough business momentum to carry you through the transitions. Look for the signals that you are at the limits of a phase and that it is time to shift gears. Have an idea in advance of how you will shift the various elements of your organization for the next phase.

An important goal over the five phases of growth is to develop the full range of capabilities and control mechanisms, as well as your own skill and wisdom to use them appropriately.

Trajectory and Momentum

When timing a change, consider the two important elements of trajectory and momentum. These are two forces that can work for you or against you. Trajectory is the direction your business is going, whether positive or negative. Momentum is how long your business will keep going in its current direction without leadership intervention. If you currently have strong momentum, little effort is needed to maintain the current level of business activity. If you have low momentum, as soon as you turn your attention away from the business, it is readily apparent.

Trajectory and momentum can work against you by making things look effective when in fact they are not. A positive trajectory and strong momentum make anyone look smart. The false impression can cause you to have greater confidence in you current practices and priorities than is justified.

On the other hand, trajectory and momentum can work for you by enabling you to make important fundamental transitions in a way that is minimally disruptive to your business. Positive trajectory and high momentum can carry your business through the difficult transitions described. It is important to time your transitions to take place when you have strong momentum from past successes. If you let the momentum dissipate before making a transition, you're more likely to fail and experience business problems. For example, after the innovation of the business has been tested in the marketplace, it is important to make a transition to the Restructuring mode quickly. If you wait until you are experiencing problems that are affecting your business, you will have lost a lot of momentum from your earlier successes.

The irony is that you should be changing when you are least driven by external forces to do so. However, this is when you find the most internal resistance to change.

The Importance of Periodic Review

As the leader, you should seek to periodically assess the structure and the culture of your organization. Determine if there is good alignment of the decision-making structure, culture, and management priorities. Consider making adjustments each year and having a major review every three years. Make incremental changes and adaptations so that there is a better fit with the current business environment, increased experience of the employees, and other developments.

Different Businesses May Take Different Paths

Many firms experience each of the five phases of development to some degree and do so in the progression shown in the road map chart. However, not all firms experience each phase to the same extent, if at all. For some companies, a particular phase may be more appropriate for a longer duration than for other companies.

The extent to which you develop all aspects of each mode depends on your situation. For example, not every new business must be based on a breakthrough innovation and therefore may not need to experience every aspect of the Concept Development phase. Franchised businesses are good examples of this exception. The new McDonald's restaurant opening up down the street will probably be able to skip full-fledged Concept Development and Foundation Development phases. The innovation underlying a McDonald's restaurant — consistent quality, low prices, and convenience — has already been developed by the parent organization, which has also engineered, simplified, and formalized their practices. Considering the difficulty of these phases, the attraction of franchises for many small businesses is not surprising.

Service-oriented firms, on the other hand, might not have the opportunity for a Rapid Market Expansion phase. Many must quickly become adapting organizations because of the low barriers to entering many service businesses and varied customer preferences that must be accommodated.

In manufacturing-oriented industries, often there is vast potential for reducing costs through better planning and refined engineering. Such a firm can be in the Planning phase for long periods and still make business gains. However, this does not mean that all manufacturing companies will always be planning organizations. Leaders should be open to all possibilities.

Recognizing Inherent Weaknesses of Each Mode

Regardless of which mode your organization is operating in, it will always face challenges in the areas in which it is inherently weak. To easily identify the blind spots or weaknesses for an organization at any given phase of its growth, simply look at the mode that is in the opposite corner of the road map chart. For example, if your organization is most like an innovating organization, its key inherent weakness is the inability to act like a planning organization, which is the mode in the opposite corner from Innovating mode in the road map.

If yours is basically a planning organization, its inherent weakness is likely to be lack of innovation and agility. A producing organization's weakness would be the inability to adapt or take on a problem-solving orientation with customers.

If yours is an adapting organization, the key weaknesses will likely be the inability to focus on one particular product or market segment and exploit it fully to gain large market share, which are the traits associated with a planning organization.

In the next chapters, you will learn about common hurdles entrepreneurs face as they work to achieve and maintain optimal alignment for their business situation. In addition, you will discover specific ways to recognize and correct alignment problems early.

Chapter 10

How Success Leads to Weakness

Two Common Ways to Get Off Track

The Natural Tendency to Cling to Past Practices

Management Style Is a Key Success Factor

Chapter 10

How Success Leads to Weakness

You now know that there are essentially five different modes of operation that correspond to five different phases of development. You have also seen that it is difficult to keep the right mode of operation aligned to the right phase of development. Now take a closer look at what happens when things go wrong because they went right.

Two Common Ways to Get Off Track

When it comes to being in the right mode at the right time, some organizations encounter two common pitfalls:

- Operating in the wrong mode, or
- Failing to achieve any successful mode of operation.

Each of these reduces an organization's effectiveness and can lead to weakness.

Operating in the Wrong Mode

Even though a firm successfully achieves any one mode of operation, it may not be the right mode for the situation. Since people tend to do what they like to do, they may select a mode of operation based primarily on personal preference as opposed to business requirements.

If an organization and a leader are more comfortable in an Innovating mode, for example, they can easily remain in that mode longer than justified by market opportunities. They may try to participate in a Rapid Market Expansion phase by operating in the Innovating mode. If so, they will fail to benefit fully from the opportunities available to them. The organization doesn't change and all past practices remain intact while opportunities for improved efficiency and larger markets are missed.

Another mistake is to change to the wrong mode for the situation. Leaders frequently adopt a mode of operation that is similar to the previous mode. For companies most comfortable in Innovation, it is easiest to move directly to the Adapting mode. Both place a high priority on creativity and flexibility and involve a high level of sensitivity to customers. Formal planning and decision structures are not strong elements of either. Serving the various niche-market segments requires customization similar to that demanded by customers during the Concept Development phase. The change from an Innovating to an Adapting mode is comfortable and easily done.

Unfortunately, this change may not be the most effective from a business point of view. If the organization does indeed have a breakthrough innovation, moving directly to an Adapting mode may not allow the focus and singular sales purpose that takes fullest advantage of the opportunity available through the Producing mode. By skipping a specialized Producing mode, the company misses some of the high profits and easy sales to buyers willing to pay a premium for its product.

The company may also miss some of the functional efficiency that would have been gained in a specialized Planning mode serving the stable market demands. By moving directly to the Adapting mode, the pragmatists and conservatives will not will have been served as quickly or effectively as they could have been.

Clearly, these very large classes of buyers should not be forsaken solely for the comfort of the organization. If you are in a highly competitive market, someone else will serve them more directly, and your company will be in a weaker competitive position.

The magnitude of the opportunity missed by skipping classes of buyers and modes of operation depends on how big a breakthrough you offer. If the organization is a high-tech venture with a major breakthrough, then much opportunity is lost by selecting a comfortable path. The cost can be high as you can see in the diagram below, which indicates the relative size of the different customer classes for a breakthrough innovation.

Classes of Buyers Within the Phases and Modes

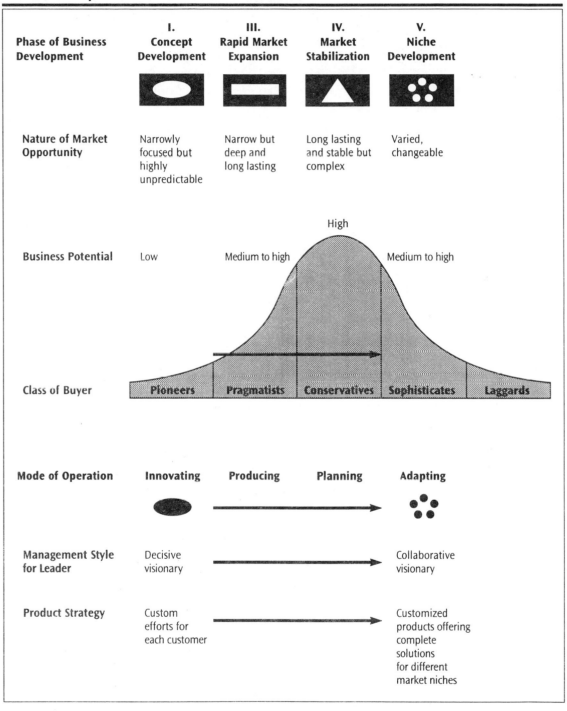

Phase of Business Development	I. Concept Development	III. Rapid Market Expansion	IV. Market Stabilization	V. Niche Development
Nature of Market Opportunity	Narrowly focused but highly unpredictable	Narrow but deep and long lasting	Long lasting and stable but complex	Varied, changeable
Business Potential	Low	Medium to high	High	Medium to high
Class of Buyer	Pioneers	Pragmatists	Conservatives	Sophisticates · Laggards

Mode of Operation	Innovating	Producing	Planning	Adapting
Management Style for Leader	Decisive visionary			Collaborative visionary
Product Strategy	Custom efforts for each customer			Customized products offering complete solutions for different market niches

While serving the pioneers and sophisticates might be fun, based on their numbers, you wouldn't want to miss the pragmatists and conservatives. The size of these classes and the demand for your product make them very attractive. Yet many entrepreneurial ventures essentially skip them. They have a preference for the Innovating and Adapting modes and simply avoid operating in a way that enables them to serve these two important classes.

Failing to Achieve Any Successful Mode

The second and more common problem organizations experience is that they fail to align their structure, culture, and control mechanisms, therefore, fail to fully develop any of the five successful modes of operation. For example, an organization may have the structure of a Planning mode, a culture similar to that of the Adapting mode, and the market strategy of the Producing mode. Such organizations seem fractured in their priorities and strategies, and in this splintered state, it is difficult for them to address the priorities of any one mode. This situation occurs

Ideal Path of Development

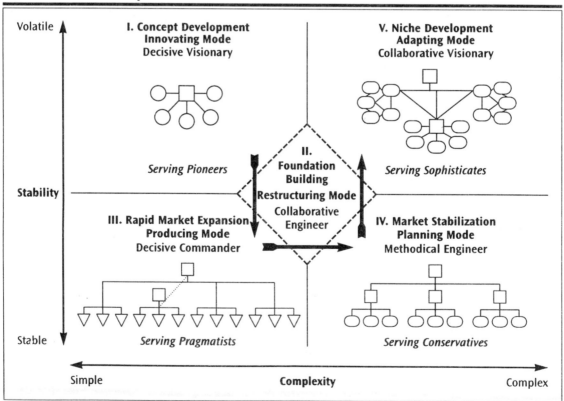

when decision makers cling to the business practices they associate with their past successes and allow other key organizational features to evolve along independent paths of least resistance.

An ideal progression through the modes is shown in the Ideal Path of Development road map. The organizational structure, management and cultural priorities, and important controls change in unison to keep pace with the changing phases of business growth and development. Unfortunately, development does not always follow the ideal path. If organizations follow the path of least resistance, as shown in the Typical Paths of Least Resistance road map, poor alignment is inevitable.

The business opportunity available to a firm that has successfully developed a valuable breakthrough innovation is to focus narrowly on selling a standardized product through a Rapid Market Expansion phase and Producing mode. Typically, however, the firm continues to place high priority on flexibility and adaptability, similar to an adapting organization. As a result, it places more emphasis on creating new innovations rather than on exploiting opportunities presented by the first innovation.

Typical Paths of Least Resistance

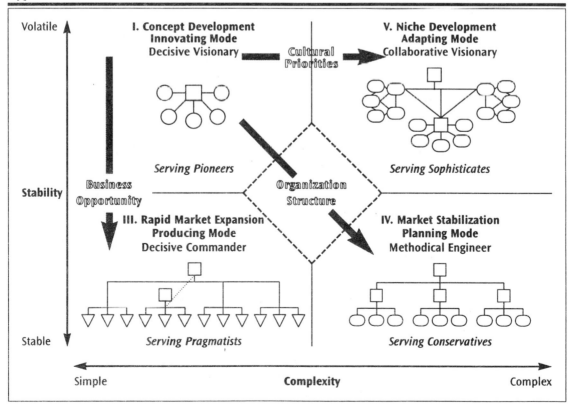

Accountability and responsibility are often poorly defined, and the firm clings to its informality. The organizational structure will become rigid because employees are most easily organized by function, with long-term employees taking the lead roles in each functional department. As more people are hired, they come in as someone's assistant rather than peer; thus the organizational layering forms. This rigid, planning-like structure prevents the firm from being as adaptable as needed, from a cultural point of view, or as aggressive and focused as the market opportunity demands. The organization becomes centralized and rigid, yet there is little accountability.

As for the nature of the work, the path of least resistance is to not change at all. Practices become institutionalized as part of the daily operation of the firm before they have been made more rational and efficient. Huts will continue to be burned down every time you want roast pork.

Your organization will avoid difficult revolutions when you follow these paths of least resistance, but the result is not positive or compelling. As a result of following these paths of least resistance, your organization will have:

- A loose, consensus-oriented culture;
- An inflexible, functionally-oriented organizational structure;
- Work practices that have not changed since they were originally pieced together in a trial-and-error fashion; and
- Employees performing their tasks according to historical practices and their own habits as opposed to coordinated teamwork.

Other paths are certainly possible, but the main point is that, when following a path of least resistance, key elements of your organization can easily fall out of alignment with the purpose of their existence.

The Natural Tendency to Cling to Past Practices

When you encounter different market environments, management situations, or technical issues that are similar to those you have successfully handled in the past, you can usually repeat past successes. However, when the situation changes and you begin to encounter problems that are subtly different in nature, the differences may not even show up on your radar screen.

It is human nature for people to try to select the problems they will face. They usually focus on problems they will be good at solving. When different types of problems surface, they can easily miss them entirely.

Unresolved problems may be small initially, but as they accumulate, they become a heavier weight on the business. As these problems grow into prominent issues, the momentum generated by past successes dissipates and the firm enters a crisis situation. There is an immediate need to restructure and manage differently in order to be effective, but there is not enough time to make the fundamental changes required. Any action is too late.

While it may sound obvious to change the company's mode of operation as the needs change, in practice it is very difficult to do so. There are several common reasons why leaders fail to initiate appropriate changes.

- People are naturally reluctant to change practices that have been successful in the past. A suggestion that something new should be done can imply that what was done before was wrong. People who have just experienced success will naturally resist this implication and point to past successes as evidence that no change is needed.

- Changes in the firm's decision making affect the power structure of the firm. Every change means someone having more power and someone else having less. Few people give up power easily, especially after the existing power structure has produced success.

- The leader may simply be more personally interested in doing things in a certain way. Especially with small entrepreneurial ventures, a leader's personal priorities often become organizational priorities. If a necessary change is contrary to the leader's preferences, the leader's personal interests may actually inhibit change.

- It may not be clear that change is needed. The clues indicating that a change is needed are often subtle and have no obvious warning signals.

- It many not be clear just what type of change is best. Even if the need for change is acknowledged, leaders need wisdom and an uncommonly broad perspective to choose the best alternative.

There is no naturally occurring force that brings together all the prerequisites for each desired mode. As a result, a deliberate effort is needed to create and maintain successful growth at each phase of development. Unlike the development of children, who mature from childhood into adolescence because of genetic programming, business growth requires conscious choice on the part of the leader. It also requires the strength to overcome the natural tendency to avoid change and take paths of least resistance.

Ironically, the more successful you are, the more you set yourself up for future trouble. Venture capitalists say that "Nothing leads to failure like success," and this true. The more you specialize your management practices in one mode, the more successful you are likely to be, and it is true that what you did led to your success. Yet the more you have specialized during one mode, the more effort you will have to expend to create the next appropriate mode of operation. The answer is not to avoid focus and specialization; if you do not specialize in a mode, you may not be effective or competitive. The answer is to be flexible.

Management Style Is a Key Success Factor

Because so much emanates from the leader, his or her style of management can become the crucial factor determining the success of the venture. However, changing one's management style is difficult — and some say impossible — because it is deeply rooted in our psychology and perhaps our biology. Yet people still have the mental capabilities that enable them to adapt to changing circumstances and to make conscious choices.

As a leader, you are faced with three courses of action when a management style other than your preferred style is needed. You can:

- Relocate yourself to a situation that is a better fit for what you do.
- Emulate the needed management style by creating the appropriate structures and setting the appropriate priorities.
- Collaborate through the intelligent and wise use of other people.

Relocate

You can bring the management style of the leader into alignment with the requirements of the situation by removing yourself or whoever is leader and bringing in someone who has a management style naturally better suited to the situation. This strategy is sometimes the only long-term solution. New leaders may be able to follow their instincts more closely to be more effective. They may also be more energized by the situation than was the earlier leader.

This approach has serious drawbacks. First, there is a loss of experience. Leaders accumulate experience and wisdom, and a loss of those assets can have a significant negative impact on the business. Second, the new leader may be well suited for just one phase and might need to be replaced later on when the situation again changes. The need that drives one leader out and another one in may be transitory, and the new leader may be no better prepared for the next important phase of growth than was the previous one.

You can also relocate the leader to a different setting within the business that responds better to the leader's style and the organization's priorities and practices. If a leader and organization excel at production, put them in charge of a business strategy that involves marketing products. A risk to depending on this strategy is that, while one can make decisions about which business to enter, businesses change in uncontrollable ways.

Unfortunately, neither of these relocation options may be consistent with the leader's or the firm's long-term interests. The organization may be reacting to short-term needs or might be assuming a greater future stability in its business situation than will actually exist.

Emulate

The second option, which is personally more difficult, is to emulate the appropriate management style by deliberately shaping the organization's structure, management and cultural priorities, and methods of control. If these variables reflect the appropriate mode, it matters less what style of management the leader actually has. To be successful in this approach, one has to become more sensitive to the requirements of the situation and manage in a more conscious manner.

For example, if you are in your element as a decisive commander taking full charge of rapid market growth, you may be very ill-at-ease when new developments require you to take on the role of collaborative visionary and suddenly you have to be people-oriented and creative. But if you do your best to emulate this style, many elements will fall into place. You can deliberately act in ways that will likely seem uncomfortable but that will help you to achieve the desired result.

To better understand this approach, consider an example from the computer industry. Macintosh and Intel-based computers running Windows are very different. The Mac has a certain computer architecture that has important strengths. Intel-based computers also have strengths. For many years, Intel compatible software would not run on Macs, but software programs are now available for the Mac that allow it to emulate an IBM machine and run IBM-compatible software. When a Mac is running the emulation software, it runs more slowly than it does when it runs Macintosh software.

So, if you're behaving in a way that is fundamentally different from your physiological makeup, you may be a little slower and you may need to be more deliberate and conscious of what you do. However, in many cases, your efforts will be sufficient to help you achieve the long-term goals of your organization.

Remember that these phases do not last forever. The period of discomfort may disappear when your business moves into a later phase.

Collaborate

Another course of action is to work with others. Create a management team that includes people with different areas of expertise and different management styles. There might be an individual who is a decisive visionary with the defiant innovation characteristic of the Concept Development phase who should take on a leadership role as the company emerges in the marketplace. Someone who is a collaborative engineer knows more instinctively what is required internally so they should take the lead during the Foundation Building phase. Someone who is a decisive commander can take the lead in the Producing mode, and so on. Using a team approach is effective, yet it can be costly and require extra coordination skills.

Wise leaders usually use some combination of emulation and collaboration. Consider all options to make sure that organizational variables are aligned with the organization's purpose, that the right modes of operation are being created. In the end, the ultimate solution lies in wisdom, conscious choice, and deliberate action. Either individually or by a team, the right options must be selected.

The next chapter describes some undesirable legacies which are symptoms of poor alignment. Understanding these challenges can help you understand where you are and where you need to go.

Chapter 11

Predictable Challenges

Battles Over Turf and Titles

You Had to Be There at the Beginning

The Office Manager Crisis

Premature Diversification

The Crisis and Rescue Cycle

Snowflakes in Waiting

The Sequel Isn't As Good As the Original

Defiant Innovation Becomes Defiant Isolation

A Flotilla of 100 Rafts

Repeated Cultural Revolutions

Assessing Vulnerability

Chapter 11

Predictable Challenges

The Innovating mode is an incredibly exciting, exhilarating time. You are developing your innovation and have begun to gather key people who can bring your product to market. In a real sense, you see the birth of your creation.

The Innovating mode is unique when compared to the other periods of growth. The structure, culture, and requirements of you as the leader may not be experienced again until you develop a new innovation. Because this time is so unique and because such dramatic changes are required as you move into the Foundation Building phase, it is common to carry over practices that were successful in the Innovating mode. These practices however, may actually turn into some very undesirable legacies.

This chapter describes 10 of the classic legacies encountered by new ventures that are inherited from a successful Innovating mode. Virtually all successful ventures encounter these challenges to some degree. These problems won't be solved overnight, but they do not have to be because the momentum of your past successes can carry you through some of them.

As an effective leader, you should be alert to these problems and correct them when the timing is right, preferably before they become unmanageable. You may be able to survive weaknesses introduced by these legacies until your business momentum is depleted, but it is important to recognize that momentum can dissipate quickly and business environments can change. Your firm may soon find itself in a situation that is less forgiving or tolerant of weakness. If this is the case, a weakened organization could prove fatal to the company or prevent it from taking advantage of new opportunities that come along.

Here is a list of 10 undesirable legacies that often create barriers to growth and success. The first six are those you will experience soon after successful innovation, and the last four appear later.

1. Battles Over Turf and Titles
2. You Had to Be There at the Beginning
3. The Office Manager Crisis
4. Premature Diversification
5. The Crisis and Rescue Cycle
6. Snowflakes in Waiting
7. The Sequel Isn't As Good As the Original
8. Defiant Innovation Becomes Defiant Isolation
9. A Flotilla of 100 Rafts
10. Repeated Cultural Revolutions

The solution to most of these situations is to shift to the appropriate mode of operation for the phase you are in. While that may sound simple enough, the hard part is being able to tune your radar so that you can identify when a problem is actually a subtle warning sign that major changes are needed.

Review these scenarios to see which ones are true for your company and to identify what needs to be changed.

Battles Over Turf and Titles

Tempers flare and members of the organization become territorial. Although the organization is still small, with 10 to 25 people, each person seems to be going a different direction. Political and personnel problems begin to take more and more management time, with the leader spending more time being referee in squabbles over who should do what and who is responsible for what. In addition, some of the staff are being overly possessive about their connections and contact with the leader. Staff become extremely sensitive to titles, and new titles are doled out to add some structure to the complex web of relationships, to reward past achievements, and to motivate staff for the future.

As a result of these problems, factions develop and the still-small organization begins to move in a surprising number of different directions. The organization's structure also develops haphazardly as employees begin to fend for themselves and become territorial with their information and influence.

Occurrence in the Developmental Cycle

This undesirable legacy typically becomes apparent at the end of the Concept Development phase. The organization may simply get too large for the Innovating mode.

Why It Is a Problem

Although battles over turf and titles may seem like superficial problems that could be addressed on a case-by-case basis, they are only symptoms of powerful underlying problems that must be solved in a comprehensive manner to allow future growth to take place.

Increased in-fighting of staff distracts the organization from external opportunities. The organization begins to splinter and move in various directions, with each faction pursuing its own interpretation of the company vision. In advanced cases, the organization becomes truly out of control.

How It Originated

This undesirable legacy is a result of the use of direct supervision for the primary method of controlling the organization during the Innovating mode. When the leader was able to daily regulate what everyone was doing, it was easy to define the roles and boundaries of every individual. As generalists, everyone was involved in every detail, and constant adjustment and refinements could be made to ensure that the organization was agile and innovative. This approach worked well as long as the organization was small.

As the company grows not everyone can have direct contact with the leader and each other. Similarly, the leader's ability to meaningfully influence everyone through direct supervision is exceeded.

A good indication that a company has exceeded the capacity to manage informally is that there are more people than can sit around a small conference table long enough to discuss everyone's status without a bathroom break. While a seven-person team, for example, can be self-regulating on an informal basis, a larger firm cannot. The time it takes for each person of a 15-member team to find out informally what everyone else is doing is more than most people in a business organization are willing to spend. As a result, a company can easily have two or three people doing something completely different, unrelated, or perhaps at odds with other people's activities.

When the leader no longer knows the details of every person's activities, the staff are left to define their positions, accountabilities, and responsibilities. When boundaries are not defined daily by the leader, people naturally become territorial and stake claim to areas they consider to be theirs. The role of the leader quickly changes from one of supervising individuals as they work together under a common vision to refereeing small groups of people who are pursuing their own agendas or second-hand interpretations of the leader's vision.

A Vancouver, Canada-based paper company of 11 employees had just hired three people to assume some of the workload of the existing staff. As the number of employees increased, the head of production, newly designated as vice president of production, was concerned that although their weekly staff meetings were getting longer, there still was not enough time for him to bring up all the issues he felt were important.

Of particular concern was the way the sales people were making promises that could not be filled by his group. This had only recently become a problem because before he was made head of production, he went on all sales calls and knew exactly what the customer wanted. With more staff members meeting customers, he now went on just a few sales calls, and problems arose with those he did not attend. He wanted to rework the sales process, but the newly designated head of the sales staff wanted to be more independent from the production group because it allowed her group to be aware of customer needs and to use a more effective sales process. Both vice presidents appealed to the CEO to settle the issue and set the priorities. The CEO realized that both parties were right and encouraged teamwork and cooperation. The problem remained despite their best efforts, and the division between sales and production grew wider.

How to Resolve the Problem

The key to addressing this problem is to understand that it is unavoidable when the organization grows as you hoped. As the number of people increases, decision making needs to be restructured to be more rational and formalized so everyone knows his or her role. The cultural shift during this time of change is dramatic, as each person's generalist capabilities, training, and interests are no longer as important as they once were. This is the essence of the Foundation Building phase, a difficult phase, but fortunately a temporary one. You can make the transition smoother by encouraging staff to take a close look at what is really going on and supporting their efforts to make their work more structured and systemized.

Most staff in successful Innovating mode organizations are generalists, so everyone can lay claim to multiple activities with some legitimacy. Sorting out the appropriate span of control for each member is difficult because it affects the sense of power and stature of everyone involved. It is for this reason that the management style of the collaborative engineer is so important during a Restructuring mode. A collaborative engineer spontaneously approaches the fundamental problems by considering the views of everyone to work out an objective, fair, and logical solution.

You Had to Be There at the Beginning

New staff take an unacceptably long period of time to understand the organization and to become effective. They are dependent on those who have been with the company since the early days. Many of the work processes and procedures have evolved organically since the business formed and have not been changed since. Any suggestions for change are strongly resisted. To understand the business, the organization, and how things get done, one almost has to have been there since it began. The original staff enjoy a special camaraderie that can appear as a clique closed to newer staff people.

Occurrence in the Developmental Cycle

This legacy typically appears after the Concept Development phase during early growth when the first new staff are hired and try to become productive.

Why It Is a Problem

Future growth will be influenced by how quickly new staff can become productive members of the organization. Longer training periods can put increased burden on other staff, and that energy could be better focused on being productive. This situation maintains the power of the early hires as the organization grows, and it contributes to structural inflexibility.

How It Originated

The first successes of the organization came from doing new things or by doing existing things in a new way. Trial-and-error was prevalent and little was documented about how things were done because documentation simply was not a priority. How things are done becomes part of the tribal lore. This legacy occurs when the organization fails to enter a period of restructuring to formalize the work processes, typical of the Restructuring mode. Consequently, tasks and processes that could be standardized are still done in unusual, informal, and ad-hoc ways.

The result is that unless employees grow up with the firm and experience first-hand the trial-and-error process, there is little hope of becoming productive quickly. New employees have to learn by osmosis, simply by being around people who were there at the beginning.

A money management firm in Denver had developed an innovative way to research small companies. The research process worked very well and was the foundation of the firm's early success. As the company attracted new clients, it hired additional analysts to help perform the research. Because no manuals existed to describe the research approach, all learning was done at the side of experienced analysts. War stories and personal philosophies conveyed the general process, but none of this information was in the form of objective and unambiguous rules for making decisions. The new analysts had to experience the process and undergo a lengthy informal apprenticeship before they could be trusted to evaluate companies independently. Unfortunately, business growth left them no other choice but to depend more and more on analysts who were not fully indoctrinated. Inevitably, their research was not thorough and investment performance suffered.

How to Resolve the Problem

The key to success in this scenario is to take a step back to differentiate what works from what doesn't. Formalize those parts of the judgment process that have stabilized and make them clearer to everyone. The benefits of this are that consistent policies and procedures are codified and become transferable. Such formalization also helps the leader and early members of the organization to identify earlier achievements. Both long-term and short-term staff benefit. Then shift to the Restructuring mode.

The Office Manager Crisis

The office manager in this scenario represents any employee who serves as the leader's right hand and manages many of the tactical and administrative issues the leader often readily delegates to them. The office manager has grown up with the firm and knows it in rich detail. They become so enmeshed with the inner workings of the company that, eventually, no decision can be made without prior consultation with the office manger. As a result, the office manager is incredibly overworked.

Quiet arguments involving the office manager begin to develop. New staff trained in accounting, for example, are dependent on the office manager to locate needed records. New staff find themselves being corrected by the office manager for violating tenets of corporate culture that are so specialized that only a long-time employee could know them. The office manager is, in effect, regulating the organization with the implied authority of the leader.

While there seems little immediate need for structuring and accessibility as long as the office manager is constantly involved, the lack of these important elements inhibits development of other staff and the organization. Eventually, the office manager's capabilities hit a ceiling and hold the company back, too.

Occurrence in the Developmental Cycle

This legacy typically becomes apparent early in the Foundation Building phase as management begins to evaluate the way staff and work processes are organized.

Why It Is a Problem

The office manager becomes both indispensable to the day-to-day operation of the firm and unable to provide the specialized knowledge and depth of skills required in the diverse areas under their control. The crisis of this legacy becomes a test of loyalty versus technical proficiency and is one of the most trying issues to resolve.

An innovative leader often assumes that everyone, including the office manager, will mature along with the growing complexity and magnitude of the job. With this well-intentioned but faulty assumption, the leader often delays providing the organization with the specialized competence it needs as it matures. This delay only widens the gap between what the situation requires and what the office manager can provide, regardless of their capability and loyalty. The longer the delay, the less likely that the office manager, as a generalist, will find a narrower role which will be both effective and satisfying. This, in turn, makes it progressively more difficult to resolve the situation.

The office manager crisis is often painful and time-consuming to resolve because it affects a loyal, long-term employee who has been instrumental to the daily operation of the firm as well as development of the other staff and the progress of the organization as a whole.

How It Originated

The typical new entrepreneur, being more concerned about innovation and big-picture issues, often hires an office manager to handle the administrative and incidental tasks. The office manager is usually one of the first people hired and therefore is a loyal generalist who is capable of performing a variety of activities. Someone who is flexible, loyal, and a jack-of-all-trades is ideal for the initial office manager.

Like many of the other employees, the office manager gains self-esteem and a sense of power from having knowledge about every detail of the organization, including past successes, failures, and the trial-and-error process that it went through. The office manager also receives a great deal of satisfaction from having direct contact with the leader.

When the office manager is hired, it is often assumed that the person will grow with the job. However, the responsibilities normally delegated to this person at the beginning of an organization's development usually change dramatically over time. It is not realistic to assume that the person hired at the beginning of the business will be able to keep pace with the changing technical requirements and the greater focus that will ultimately be required. Nor is it reasonable to assume that someone who is motivated and energized by generalist activities will be satisfied by more narrowly defined jobs later on.

Office managers sometimes believe that, as generalists, they will have no place in a more specialized company. Efforts to specialize are sometimes interpreted as a threat to their positions.

A San Diego firm started with just a few employees. Among the first people hired was an energetic young man who was willing to undertake any task. He started with bookkeeping and then progressed to be the head of administration. Due to his energy and willingness to work long hours and because of the small size of the organization, he was involved in every aspect of the company's operations. He eventually had three people working for him and performing tasks suitable for entry-level staff. He became so entwined with the company that the president said that he was actually the true president, and that if something had to be done, he could get it done.

He maintained strong control over his team and did not allow them to progress to higher-level tasks. In addition, he felt threatened by people who were developing greater competence, and he withheld information that would enable them to act independently without his involvement. He was naturally the one most threatened by efforts to define and differentiate his activities, and he resisted in quiet but meaningful ways. Somehow every decision had to involve him, and if someone cut him out of the loop, they did not get the information they needed. If they failed, he would then step in with the needed information to reaffirm that progress was more certain with him than without him. For the most part, this actually was true over the short-term; when he was not involved, things did not go smoothly or quickly. Although it may sound as though he had bad intentions, he did not. Insisting upon being involved in everything was a key to early success. He was also seen as a parent figure to many in the organization and was a tremendous resource. His resistance to change was simply to protect the practices and cultural values he felt had been responsible for past successes.

However, the growth being experienced by the firm required greater functional expertise than any generalist could provide, regardless of his or her energy. In this case, the leader was among the last to realize that the office manager's role had become an impediment to growth. The intense bond of loyalty made it difficult for the leader to see the broader picture and longer-term business needs or that the real needs of the company in specialized areas like accounting, personnel, and production had progressed beyond what the office manager could provide. Once his job had been separated into its different functions, he was not suited for any specialized area. He ultimately left the company.

How to Resolve the Problem

Try to make a special effort early on to plan a career path for the office manager and provide the training they need to become more of a specialist. As the leader, you can initiate this plan before the organization has developed too far in terms of requiring technical specialization. The manager can then specialize in an area well-suited to his or her interests and capabilities and to the organization's needs. Unfortunately, many office managers find the more narrow focus and requirement to develop a greater level of technical expertise beyond their interests. What they may like most are the breadth of activities and the exposure to all aspects of the company that they previously enjoyed.

The situation in this undesirable legacy may not reach a crisis level if the business environment and concepts of the company are strong enough to support the office manager in a more generalist role that still allows other staff to develop. The economics of your situation may not allow this option, but it is often preferable to losing the manager's experienced presence.

Premature Diversification

The firm sees itself as a fount of new ideas and innovations while riding the success of its early innovation. The leaders are enjoying the exhilaration of creative innovation and want to keep doing more of it. Any hint that some effort should go to internal management issues is met with scorn. "Our little company is not going to become a stuffy, old bureaucracy," they vow. As a result, the company devotes its collective energy to developing a diverse product line.

Meanwhile, competing firms pick up their innovative ideas and exploit them more broadly and effectively. Without a solid revenue stream from any of its products, the firm begins to strain under the burden of developing and promoting its numerous products. The innovators' initial surge of energy begins to dissipate as fast as their start-up funds.

Occurrence in the Developmental Cycle

This legacy usually appears after the Concept Development phase or the Foundation Building phase when the organization should be moving into the Rapid Market Expansion phase using the Producing mode.

Why It Is a Problem

The business that is missed by failing to serve the pragmatists in the Rapid Market Expansion phase can be immense. Many firms that do move successfully into the Rapid Market Expansion phase using the Producing mode benefit greatly from a sizable steady income. With the revenue and stability provided by taking full advantage of the initial innovation, they can support continued development of the first product and the organization as well as other innovations later on.

How It Originated

A natural tendency exists for a leader to continue doing what they like to do, and the leader of a successful Innovation-phase firm usually prefers to create and be innovative. Even if they have gone through the Foundation Building phase, there is a natural desire to continue or quickly resume creative activity.

By continuing to place a high priority on innovation, they jeopardize a small organization's ability to develop the first innovation to its maximum potential. A leader may prematurely divert the organization's intellectual and financial resources to another innovation. This dilution of resources results in an array of ideas with little potential for major market success.

A Seattle-based manufacturing company developed a fuel pump for the aerospace industry that was recognized as the best designed and most rugged in its class. The company had built a better mousetrap, but the world was not beating a path to its door. The firm's leadership knew of this problem and considered it important, but most of their time was spent developing new products based on the technology of the original ground-breaking fuel pumps.

Despite the company's great reputation, sales of the fuel pump were not as high as those of competitors. A competing firm not noted for innovation had emulated the functions of the pump and aggressively marketed and supported its product in the marketplace. Soon the competing pump dominated the market.

The leaders of the firm felt the market had been taken from them, but in fact, they had failed to take it when they had the chance. Instead, they chose to diversify to other innovative products rather than to focus on growth and expansion. Their products in general were viewed as innovative but less reliable and costlier than competitors' products. While it was not a conscious decision, their interests and desire to repeat past successes drew them to the mentality associated with the Innovation mode. Despite its innovative success, the company unfortunately never achieved the business success justified by their innovations or their expectations, and eventually the company's growth leveled off.

How to Resolve the Problem

At the end of the Foundation Building phase, your management should take a close look at the business potential for your product and determine if a Rapid Market Expansion phase is available to you. If so, attempt to move into a Producing mode to capture as much of the market as possible. Even if for a short period, experience in this phase introduces a more focused element into the culture and structure of the organization.

Although given the volatile nature of the markets for new ventures, it is sometimes not easy to select the single best product or service accurately; then you can identify more than one, in order to diversify selection risk. However, make sure that the selection of multiple products is based on a business need rather than a cultural bias. The greater the number of products needed to reduce business risk to a reasonable level, the less likely you are actually in a Rapid Market Expansion phase. If more products need to be offered to maintain a reasonable level of business risk, consider a Planning or Adapting mode.

Remember that during a Producing mode there is little customization and the leader is focused externally into the market. This is very different from the cultures of the Innovating and Restructuring modes in which customization and internal focus, respectively, are characteristic.

The Crisis and Rescue Cycle

The entrepreneurial leader is still the main mover and shaker in their young company. However, they are beginning to feel overwhelmed by the numerous responsibilities that continue to increase as company growth picks up. Someone suggests that delegating work to others is the answer. So the leader immediately delegates work and decision making to the staff.

The situation deteriorates shortly after delegation takes place. Details are overlooked, errors are made, and the essence of the vision is not fulfilled. Eventually the leader must return to the scene in a rescue operation. The leader's return reinforces the idea that they are absolutely indispensable to the day-to-day activities of the business. Once again the leader eventually becomes overwhelmed and bored at the same time.

Occurrence in the Developmental Cycle

This undesirable legacy becomes apparent during or after the Concept Development phase.

Why It Is a Problem

This crisis and rescue cycle prevents the leader from addressing new issues as well as hinders staff from developing their capabilities. Throughout the crisis and rescue cycle, the organization makes mistakes, people overlook details, and execution of decisions is poor. Organizational systems that have been initiated do not become self-sufficient, so the leader cannot devote attention to other matters. The leader must fight rearguard action rather than being focused on the new battles for growth that lie ahead.

How It Originated

This undesirable legacy is based on the informal nature of decision making and the use of supervision as the main method of control during the Innovation phase. Responsibilities and accountabilities are not well defined, and infrastructure is lacking in important areas such as accounting, decision making, and planning. In addition, there is a lack of specialization in responsibilities for employees and an overly complex process for getting the work done. All these make it difficult to delegate successfully.

It often happens that an entrepreneurial leader gets bored with the day-to-day running of the business and wants to start something else. They like to believe that their loyal team can handle the future. Instead of shepherding their business through a Foundation Building phase that will enable the team to operate more independently, the leader suddenly just decreases involvement. The natural distaste successful innovative leaders have for foundation building makes this scenario all too common. Mundane business issues and management do not hold their attention as does pursuing a new innovation.

It is common to hear that entrepreneurs don't delegate. In fact, they do delegate and do so frequently and repeatedly. Unfortunately, however, they tend to delegate abruptly and with little preparation. All else being equal, decisive visionaries favor either complete personal control or complete delegation; it's all or nothing. The individual to whom they delegate is typically not adequately prepared for the autonomy they have been given. The delegatee goes from being data gatherer to decision maker in the blink of an eye. Without a structure to support them and a logical method of accomplishing objectives, the delegatee is in a no-win situation. Inevitably, they make poor decisions and misjudgments, and the leader must come in to rescue the situation. Finding that decisions have not been made the way they would have made them, the leader then takes back all of the decision-making authority and control.

This sequence of events reconfirms to the leader that they really shouldn't have delegated in the first place. Faced with an organization out of control, they put forth a super-human effort and try to repeat the success of the early days by reasserting tight central control.

However, it is not possible to maintain tight personal control in a large organization over long periods of time. The leader soon tires and decides to try delegating again, particularly after a period when there have been no problems. They again reduce their involvement. Without real preparation for delegation, another crisis develops and they are forced again to return to save the day.

A Denver firm experienced a series of crisis and rescue cycles as the leader attempted to start another business activity. She was a hands-on leader who thrived on the thrill of startups. About three years after starting one business, she believed that her team had learned the ropes. They had worked together all that time, and although there was no formal training because everyone had seen every part of the business, she thought that any one of her staff could replace her. The truth was that she was getting a bit bored and dreamed of the start-up phase. She decided to begin another business. Once the decision was made, she felt the rush of excitement as she contemplated the new strategy. As soon as this occurred, however, she was completely absent from the first business.

The remaining team attempted to keep the first business going. They were successful for a while. They tried to make decisions in a way that was consistent with the absent leader's views, but they were simply guessing about what she would have done and tried to keep doing what had been done in the past. Unfortunately, none of those remaining had an intensely-held vision of the organization's purpose. Most of their past experience had been following the leader's guidance, not working independently. While they kept doing what they had done in the past, they lost track of why they did things that way. Because of this, they had no way to tell from the changes in the business how their internal practices should be revised. None had been in a position to see the overall big picture.

Ultimately, business problems emerged. Seeing the situation, the leader appeared on the scene to guide the organization through the difficult period, setting a bold new vision for people to focus on and to guide their activities. She again became involved in every detail. But when the short-term problems were solved, the leader disappeared and the cycle began again.

Because the leader was committed to the success of both efforts, the problems experienced by the firm never became critical. However, while both businesses were just successful enough to stay in business, the crisis and rescue cycle became a full-time preoccupation. The leader did not have the time to address the fundamental problems of either business, and neither grew. The leader and her companies were trapped in a perpetual survival mode and could not prepare for future growth.

How to Resolve the Problem

The crisis and rescue cycle can be broken. When there is no crisis at hand, the leader should take a step back and first go through the Foundation Building phase using the Restructuring mode. This enables the leader to identify decision-making resources, requirements, and objectives and to deliberately set the employees up for success rather than for failure.

Snowflakes in Waiting

A speck of dust or pollen is often needed to form a snowflake. Without something to crystallize around, the water vapor fails to form into snowflakes and remains suspended. Just as water molecules gather around a speck of dust to create a snowflake, the leader acts as the object around which the members of an innovating organization gather. If the leader opts out of this role for any reason, there is no central force or clear vision to guide decisions.

Without the leader, what was once a decisive and responsive organization stagnates. People avoid making decisions. All required information is collected and assembled, but no one brings the issue to a point of decision and determines who will do this and who will do that to accomplish the objectives. Weakness arises not so much because wrong decisions are made but because no decisions are made and little action is taken. Decision making is slow and tentative.

Occurrence in the Developmental Cycle

This hazard first appears after the Innovating mode when the organization should be developing a more formal and expanded decision-making structure that assigns accountability and responsibility to its various members.

Why It Is a Problem

Decisions do not get made, and the company fails to respond quickly to opportunities and problems.

How It Originated

This legacy results from the leadership allelopathy of the Innovating mode. As described earlier, leadership allelopathy refers to the beneficial way an innovating leader helps maintain the singular vision for the firm by seeking people who are loyal and support the vision as opposed to having independent visions of their own. These members of the organization are rewarded for their continued loyalty to the leader's vision. As discussed earlier, allelopathy can be positive as long as the effect is reduced once the vision has been validated.

In the Innovating mode, everyone has a vote, but the only vote that counts is the leader's. Everyone participates in all decisions and there is a sense of consensus decision making, but in reality, there is just one decision maker: the leader. Others are loyal to the vision of the leader, gather information, and participate in discussion, but the leader calls for an end to discussion and authorizes action.

When the involvement of the leader decreases, the leader no longer plays the role of the speck of dust around which information gathers in order for the decisions to be made. The second generation performs just as before, but the decisions do not get made as quickly or effectively.

A New York City money management organization had experienced several years of good performance, had accepted some new, large accounts, and now managed several billion dollars. The leader was an insightful and intuitive decision maker who had created the firm four years previously and had personally hired key staff. Each person was a generalist, and everyone participated in all decisions and openly shared their views about what should be done. Because of the firm's success, the leader decided to start a new investment venture to take advantage of clients' interest in similar services offered by a competing company.

The staff took over primary control of the existing investment process. Because the investment disciplines had been fully developed, the leader believed that it was time to step aside and let some of the other members of the organization assume stronger roles in order to pursue their career interests. The leader reduced his involvement, but there were few other changes. The staff and the leader continued to have meetings every week to discuss recent economic news and its impact on which stocks they bought and sold.

Unfortunately, as time passed, the company's performance began to deteriorate; they were not doing as well as they had been previously. When they studied the situation more closely, they realized that their decisions were safer than they had been in the past. They were slower to make bold decisions, and the decisions they made quickly tended to be conservative. Competing firms were simply faster and more insightful.

To promote faster decisions, the firm assigned one person to be the central decision maker. But it was difficult to determine which of the four peers should be promoted above the others to become leader. People who had enjoyed being peers and having the same role in decision making resisted this change. When one was selected for the role, it was discovered that his temperament did not lend itself to the role of being the visionary. The person was uncomfortable in the role and tried hard to be as collaborative as possible so that others would support the process.

Despite all attempts, the organization could not operate effectively without the original central leader. Not only did attempts to improve the decision-making structure go against the one-for-all culture that was so prized but the improvements also seemed to require more independence of thought than the staff could provide. They had been hired for loyalty to the vision of the leader and had developed in an era of leadership allelopathy; therefore, their ability to function as independent decision-makers was reduced.

How to Resolve the Problem

There are three main ways to avoid the phenomenon of snowflakes in waiting. The first is to determine that the Innovating mode is the right one for your business at this time and therefore decentralized decision making is not appropriate. If this is the case, the leader should stay involved, and the organization should avoid growth. They can outsource as many activities as possible to maintain a narrow focus of efforts.

The second way to avoid this legacy is to manage the ebb of leadership allelopathy and allow staff to develop their own capabilities as independent decision makers earlier than needed. It is important to remember that, overall, allelopathy is good for an entrepreneurial venture. It enables a young firm to be highly focused, innovative, and responsive to quickly changing opportunities. However, as soon as an innovation is developed that will support extensive growth, allelopathy should be reduced. As you begin to see that the Concept Development phase and the Innovating mode are no longer appropriate for your business, begin to hire people who are more independent as opposed to those of high loyalty required early in the Innovating mode.

A third way for you to avoid the snowflakes in waiting scenario is to begin early to develop formal decision processes that guide people along a productive path without your close supervision. Begin to differentiate the roles of members of your organization to allow greater specialization and depth of understanding. Assign accountability and authority in unambiguous terms early, before you step out of the picture so everyone can become accustomed to their new roles. Then, let your top managers make decisions, even if you disagree.

The Sequel Isn't As Good As the Original

After the company's initial breakthrough product was introduced in the marketplace, it was extremely successful. The company got a lot of momentum from the first burst of sales.

Now that things are settling down and the product is beginning to mature, management decides to undertake the next major innovation as a way to rejuvenate the business. They decide to introduce a sequel to the initial ground-breaking innovation with the hopes that the new innovation will rewrite the rules of the industry, just as their first product did. They figure success is assured. After all, the firm can now provide all the support and guidance lacking when the first innovation was done on a shoestring budget.

Unfortunately, the sequel does not rewrite the rules of the industry and is, sadly, notably mediocre.

Occurrence in the Developmental Cycle

This undesirable legacy is typically encountered in companies that have moved past the Foundation Building and Rapid Market Expansion phases.

Why It Is a Problem

Products have life cycles, and innovation is needed to allow the organization to survive, build revenue, and continue growing. If subsequent innovations are mediocre, continued growth is jeopardized.

How It Originated

When the sequel is not as good as the first, it is sometimes because the second product or service was developed using a mode of operation other than the Innovating mode. Instead, the organization uses the mode currently used for the business of the first innovation, wherever it is in its developmental cycle. Unfortunately, the phase of development for the first innovation may no longer be Concept Development. It may have moved on to the Rapid Market Expansion or Market Stabilization phase. The second innovation may therefore lack the spark of the first.

The Producing and Planning modes are poorly suited to breakthrough innovation because the committees and formal plans put in place to develop and produce the first innovation do not lend themselves to creativity. While committees tend to make defensible decisions, decisions that can stand up to the scrutiny of a group discussion, these decisions often represent consensus, which is the lowest common denominator of the views expressed. Individuals, on the other hand, are more capable of making decisions based primarily on insight or intuition, and it is for this reason that breakthrough innovations usually bear the mark of a single individual's vision.

To achieve breakthrough innovation, an individual must be able to cut across a company's functional divisions and must be allowed no distractions while immersed in information relating to the innovation. Unfortunately, such far-reaching individual autonomy is not consistent with the formalized structures and practices associated with successful producing or planning organizations. Therefore, it is very difficult for a large company to foster breakthrough innovation. To overcome this hurdle, some firms create a so-called skunk works operation to develop an innovation. This means creating an innovating organization within, or alongside of, the larger organization, making it possible for a team to work outside of the structural and cultural impediments of the rest of the company.

A California manufacturer of computers hoped to repeat the staggering success of its first computer. The first computer was developed in a garage, and serendipity played a big part in their successes; they believed they were lucky.

For their second computer, management decided to research the target market segments and systematically profile the various needs and benefits sought by those buyers. They would then determine how to market the product effectively to each buyer segment. They planned to use an external manufacturer to develop the prototype, and all final design decisions would have the full support of the organization. A skilled project manager was brought in to oversee the process and ensure it went smoothly and efficiently. The company allocated several million dollars to the project to make sure that it was adequately funded.

The project went ahead as planned. The company developed a design that met the needs of the target market segments and was approved by the leadership of the firm. They developed a prototype and subjected it to the review of key staff in charge of various functions, such as production, marketing, support, and research and development. Each person reviewed the prototype against a checklist of issues that were raised by members of their groups. The prototype was approved with just a few changes, although some staff members expressed concerns about the cost of production. Some of the required manufacturing techniques were new to the firm, but the conclusion was that these details could be worked out later when it was time to start production.

After several months, the computer was introduced to the market with great fanfare as the rightful successor to the company's first computer. Market expectations were high, and the machine was reviewed carefully by potential customers. After some initial excitement in the product, however, interest faded. The new computer failed to create a new market segment and was not clearly superior to existing computers in established segments. The computer didn't ever grab the market and was eventually discontinued.

In retrospect, they realized that the computer embodied some very creative ideas but that the overall execution lacked the bold purity of thought characteristic of their initial computer and of competitors' successful machines. The process was too complicated, and too many design changes had been made to satisfy various participants in the development process. In addition, they realized that no one person had overseen all details, so the execution of the original intent had been poor. For example, when the manufacturing department found that they could not easily make what was intended, they substituted a different technique. Throughout planning and development, there had been many such decisions, and the final product embodied those compromises. The strategy fell short because the process of developing breakthrough innovation is largely intuitive and individualistic and cannot be delegated to others, especially to a committee.

How to Resolve the Problem

To avoid the weak sequel legacy, recognize that the Concept Development phase requires a special situation, an innovating organization. Set aside a small team and allow them to focus on a limited number of issues. Immerse them in information and give them freedom to create.

Defiant Innovation Becomes Defiant Isolation

When a new young company makes a big splash in the marketplace with a bold innovation, it may make the headlines and be the talk of the town for a time. This taste of fame can be heady stuff, enough to convince the leaders that their defiance of the norm is an effective part of their company's culture.

In this scenario, members of the organization refuse to listen to and understand what is taking place in the marketplace and to modify their own actions accordingly. They are skeptical of anything outside of their own four walls. They are also insensitive to the marketplace, continuing to believe that they know more about what the customer wants than the customer does. While that fact proved true in the beginning, they make the mistake of assuming it would remain true forever.

Occurrence in the Developmental Cycle

This undesirable legacy becomes particularly apparent and problematic when the organization should be moving into the Adapting mode.

Why It Is a Problem

If this scenario continues, the company can become out of touch with the market and its own customers. It can fail to keep up with the development of the very market it helped to create or fail to take advantage of the market's demand for variations of its initial product.

How It Originated

This situation emerges from the attitude of defiance that was a necessary component of the Innovating mode. Defiance of conventional wisdom was a crucial ingredient in the creation of a breakthrough innovation, allowing people to believe they could create a new product or business where none had existed before. During the period of breakthrough innovation, an insightful and effective entrepreneur often defies prevailing practices and techniques and the articulated demands of the market. Unfortunately, defiant innovation of the early days can easily atrophy into a defiant isolation later on, as the decision makers continue to withdraw from external events. They may even become insensitive to developments in the market sometimes created by introduction of their own product.

This defiance can sometimes be seen as a patronizing attitude when a company gives the impression that it is so far ahead of the market that there is no real need to listen to what the customers say.

Defiant isolation is a problem particularly when the company's early breakthrough innovations become part of the conventional wisdom. Once the ground-breaking innovation has been accepted and integrated into the marketplace, the market will give ample feedback about the product and how it can be improved and customized to meet more specialized needs. Companies suffering from defiant isolation often don't hear this feedback or don't take it seriously when they do. As a result, they can miss significant opportunities.

A Boston-based company specializing in medical devices was first to introduce an innovative blood-sampling device that changed the market. The device sold well, and several other firms introduced copycat products. The firm took pride in creating a new market segment and held itself out as the industry leader. The company was confident that the fundamental merit of the device would serve it well in terms of business growth. The company devoted attention to producing a large volume of the devices and then going on to the next great breakthrough. However, the buyers of the device were diverse and found many different ways to use it. Demand for customized applications was so great that several competing companies introduced products to be used in conjunction with the device that made it better suited to various medical situations.

To the market, the initial version of the product was beginning to appear out-of-date and not versatile enough. Competing firms seemed to bend over backwards to work with customers on how the device might be modified to make it better suited to their needs. However, although the market was taking off, the Boston company's business was not keeping up.

How to Resolve the Problem

In the Innovating mode, you can lecture to the market. Later on, you must listen to the market. You must make a conscious cultural shift from the defiant innovation approach typical of a successful Concept Development phase to the more market-driven focus of the Niche Development phase.

To minimize the risk of isolation, the innovative staff of a larger organization needs to maintain direct contact with the outside world and be free from organizational responsibilities that insulate them from it. Keep innovating departments small and flexible. If the firm becomes large, allow sub-units to develop and give them the autonomy to go outside the firm for information and research.

A Flotilla of 100 Rafts

This company was especially good at adding more staff and introducing new lines of business, but little cooperation existed among the various business units. The organization and its business had become overdiversified. None of the lines of business was developed to its full potential, with few of them moving beyond the Concept Development phase. Some observant employees suspected that two different business lines within the company were serving the same segment of the market yet they had little idea of what the other was doing. Redundancies and overlapping functions existed, but the businesses remained separate.

Overall growth of the firm was achieved by adding new lines of business. Instead of being a coordinated single venture seeking to maximize its overall business, it was a collection of boutique businesses, with few becoming well developed and little synergy among the entities. Rather than being a fleet of synchronized ships able to move in a coordinated fashion to meet objectives, the organization was a flotilla of rafts moving with the currents, unable to focus direction and efforts.

Occurrence in the Developmental Cycle

This undesirable legacy is common among larger firms that operate in business environments with many opportunities and occurs in later stages of the development cycle.

Why It Is a Problem

Overall growth of the firm is limited by barriers imposed by each business line's inability to expand past a start-up stage of growth. The risk is high that all lines need to be restructured, but the firm may not have the business momentum to sustain the restructuring needed to become a better established organization.

How It Originated

The flotilla of rafts has its roots in a bias toward innovation and opportunism characteristic of innovating organizations. Starting new businesses becomes ingrained as part of the culture. Developing plans, focus, and reliability are not.

―――――――――

A software company in the Northeast had so many different businesses that the firm was unable to create a single chart that reflected them all. Even long-time employees found it difficult to keep up with what the company did. Some business units were sizable and easily identified; others were small startups that were starved for corporate attention. As an information-based industry, its change was rapid when the computer revolution hit with full force. Because the firm consisted of many smaller sub-businesses, it had been able to benefit from many small changes in the industry.

The leadership of the firm, however, concluded that a major threat lay on the horizon. New competitors affiliated with larger companies had decided to be major players in the company's main line of business, and these competitors had the financial muscle to dominate the market unless the firm responded quickly and directly. The leadership concluded that to protect their traditional businesses they needed to develop deeper capabilities and be able to respond more quickly to large-scale challenges.

Despite their accurate recognition of the competitive threat and the selection of a suitable strategy, they were unable to coordinate their flotilla of rafts to withstand the competitive challenge. Under the strain of this competitive pressure, the firm's major lines of business no longer grew rapidly. While some in the firm were happy they had many businesses to fall back on, none of these side businesses was able to support the size of the total organization. The reduced growth of the major business lines forced the firm to cut loose some of the rafts, or business units, and let them fend for themselves. The firm was no longer a high-growth firm, and most of the business units that were cut adrift failed.

―――――――――

How to Resolve the Problem

Do not allow all your business units to run out of momentum at the same time. To address this problem, identify the business units that have the greatest opportunity for growth. If they currently have high business momentum and can sustain a period of restructuring, consider doing so. They can be restructured and developed from makeshift rafts to coordinated ships.

Repeated Cultural Revolutions

One way for an organization to deal with the need for growth and flexibility is by frequent changes in leadership. Through these cultural revolutions, the entire company can quickly leap from one business phase directly into another, seemingly overnight, and yet retain the quality of a homogeneous culture.

Entire management structures and philosophies are revamped as the organization moves through different phases. Because there is a relatively complete purging of prior influences, diverse ideas fail to accumulate, and what does persist is persecuted. Rather than becoming more capable of handling any mode of operation required, the organization is still as one dimensional as it was early on. In fact it becomes more rigid instead of more flexible. Its collective memory about how to create an innovating organization, for example, is minimal.

The new leaders for a particular phase have previously achieved some success practicing a certain approach to management, usually at another organization, and so are adamant that their approach is most successful now and forever. Circumstances inevitably change, however, and their time will end.

Occurrence in the Developmental Cycle

This undesirable legacy can be seen at any phase of development.

Why It Is a Problem

The revolutions are disorienting, and the purges expel people, cultural values, attitudes, and practices that may be needed in the future. Little continuity develops in organizations that change leadership too frequently. Cultural values that should be adopted from each phase are often not given the credit they deserve and are not available for use in future situations as needed.

How It Originated

A change in leadership is meant to bring the management style of the leader more in line with business requirements. A new leader comes in and is sometimes successful. Old cultural values are abandoned for the new and more recently successful ones.

Unfortunately, the new leader may be suitable for only the current situation and be no better prepared than the previous one for the series of changes that will be required as the organization evolves. If the new leader is good for only one phase and for a specialized organization, there is greater risk that future leadership changes will be needed as the organization matures. This sets the stage for a series of cultural purges that can be unnecessarily disruptive and may not bring about the results needed.

The new leaders often believe they have the best approach now and forever, but they may be well suited only to the transitory situation. What is in fact simply a phase is interpreted as a permanent new era requiring an entirely new way of doing things. However, the circumstances of the organization can change and render the new leaders just as ineffective as the old. While they may be good leaders, they may not have developed the wisdom to truly understand the requirements of the present situation as it relates to future ones.

A company near Salt Lake City became keenly aware that it had to change. The company was started by a charismatic visionary who was mainly interested in pursuing basic research in the field for which they built software. Under his leadership, the firm pursued research grants from the government for software development. As it grew, it became unable to survive on the sales being generated by its various lines of business. When the market became more competitive for the type of software it developed and produced, the company had to improve efficiency and focus in order to compete.

At the insistence of the board of directors, leadership of the company was transferred to someone who was more focused on marketing and sales. This new leader successfully developed a structure and culture consistent with those objectives. In the process, however, several members of the organization who had been key contributors in the past were forced out or chose to leave because the company was no longer consistent with their interests. The remaining staff withstood the difficult process of changing cultural priorities and the shifting power structure of the organization. The changes were time consuming and required a great deal of effort on everyone's part. However, the changes that took place were expensive and deep and, unfortunately, made with the conviction that what was done in the past would not be needed in the future.

After success in expanding their presence in the software market, they found that their software programs needed rejuvenation and additional development. The original spark had faded, and their product was looking dated. Unfortunately, the staff ideally suited for quickly and effectively re-igniting the spark had left. New people were hired to enhance the software, but they did not have the needed depth of experience with the company, and the resulting product did not have the feel and function of the original. Customers whose own business practices had evolved around the original product were dissatisfied. Eventually, the company began to lose the loyalty of its customers.

How to Resolve the Problem

The way to meet this challenge is for the leader to allow and promote greater flexibility and to acknowledge that different management approaches are needed at different times. If the valuable insights and experiences of prior leaders can be retained while accommodating other kinds of leadership, the firm will be more successful.

Begin early to assemble a management team for your company. Diversity is important for keeping a company vibrant and successful in the long run, so value the history and diversity of your company while understanding what types of leaders are needed through different phases of development.

To manage the various phases of development effectively, an organization requires a wide range of management behavior. It is best to find people who can complement each other. This is one of the main reasons for forming an organization, to bring together people with different technical and interpersonal capabilities to form a unit that is greater than the sum of its parts.

Assessing Vulnerability

The Vulnerability to Undesirable Legacies chart on the next page gives you a way to assess your business' vulnerability to the various undesirable legacies. It is based on your company's phase of business development, the number of people involved in the organization, and the decision style of the dominant leader.

The chart has three main sections of columns, A, B, and C. Section A indicates the phase of your business. Do your best to determine objectively

Vulnerability to Undesirable Legacies

Undesirable Legacies	Concept Devel.	Found. Building	R. Mrkt. Expans.	Market Stabili.	Niche Devel.	1–9	10–15	15–25	25–50	50+	Directive	Analytic	Conceptual	Behavioral	SCORE
I. Classic Legacies of Each Mode															
Reluctance to Demystify the Magic – Innovating	X	X					X	X	X		X		X		
Perpetual Introspection – Restructuring		X	X						X	X		X		X	
Lemmings to the Sea – Producing			X	X					X	X	X				
Stuck in an Obsolete Rut – Planning				X	X				X	X	X	X			
Distinction without Difference – Adapting					X				X	X			X	X	
II. Legacies of Innovation Appearing Earlier															
Battles over Turf and Titles		X	X	X	X		X	X			X		X		
You Had to Be There at the Beginning		X	X	X	X		X	X				X	X	X	
The Office Manager Crisis		X	X	X	X		X	X			X	X	X	X	
Premature Diversification		X	X	X	X			X	X	X	X		X	X	
The Crisis and Rescue Cycle		X	X	X	X			X	X		X		X		
Snowflakes in Waiting		X	X	X	X			X	X	X	X		X		
III. Legacies of Innovation Appearing Later															
The Sequel Isn't As Good As the Original			X	X	X				X	X	X	X	X	X	
Defiant Innovation Becomes Isolation			X	X	X				X	X	X	X	X		
Flotilla of 100 Rafts					X					X		X	X	X	
Repeated Cultural Revolutions			X	X	X				X	X	X	X	X	X	

the phase of your business' development. Also, keep in mind that your company may consist of several different businesses. Focus on only one business as you go through this exercise.

Section B is the size of your organization in terms of the number of people involved in decision making and operations. If you are evaluating a unit within a larger organization, you will probably encounter the undesirable legacies at a smaller size than listed in this section.

Section C is the decision style of the dominant leader of the business. The dominant leader is one who sets the tone and priorities for the organization and may be you or a predecessor. To determine your decision style, use Appendix A as a guide.

Within each of these three sections, circle the column under the description that best fits your situation. For example, you might circle the Rapid Market Expansion phase column in Section A, the 50+ column in Section B, and the conceptual and directive columns in section C.

Then for each undesirable legacy, read across each row from left to right, add the numbers that appear in the columns you circled, and total the number of Xs in the score column. The higher scores indicate the undesirable legacies you are most vulnerable to.

Chapter 12

Survival Tips

Know Yourself

See Your Situation Objectively

Allow Objectives to Diverge

Look for Deeper Issues

Use Business Momentum Wisely

Anticipate Changes

Work Through Others

Sculpt the Culture of Your Organization

Broaden Your Range of Skills

Make Natural Tendencies Pay

Chapter 12

Survival Tips

The most important asset you have as the leader of an entrepreneurial venture is wisdom. Wisdom is what separates the truly exceptional leader from the one who just happens to be at the right place at the right time. Lucky leaders can come into a situation that happens to require their preferred way of managing. To be effective over long periods of time and in different situations, however, a leader must know when to champion different priorities, even when they are not those which are personally most comfortable. You must be able to determine the right moment to make the change prior to when the need is critical. You must have the wisdom to know when some discomfort associated with change will produce greater future benefits.

The survival tips in this chapter describe 10 personal and organizational disciplines gathered from successful leaders over many years. You can take advantage of these insights and benefit from the experience of these wise individuals.

Know Yourself

To effectively manage your growing organization through the challenges that confront it, you must first understand your own biases. Think about what work situations you find most interesting. Consider the types of situations in which you have been most successful. Is there a relationship between the situations you prefer and those in which you are most successful? Think about what situations you find boring and what situations have been less than successful for you. Is there some relationship between the situations you find boring or uncomfortable and those in which you are less successful?

The decision style inventory found in Appendix A is a valuable tool for shedding light on some of your biases. It can show you how you compare to those who are naturally well suited to lead an organization during each of the phases of development. It can help you discover what phase you are naturally well suited for, as well as which phase you will be most uncomfortable in.

While a leader's management style is important, other factors such as wisdom, flexibility, and energy can ultimately be more important. Flexibility allows you to change organizational priorities at different times, to fit the method to the moment. It can be helpful to assess your own level of flexibility for a particular leadership role. For example, you may be very comfortable setting priorities for breakthrough innovation but less willing to shift priorities to develop existing ideas that are far from breakthrough.

How much energy you are willing to expend is also important. You may have the wisdom and the flexibility but may not be able to provide the energy required to promote and implement a change in priorities.

See Your Situation Objectively

When you look at your business situation, see it for what it really is, as opposed to what you would like it to be. What people see often is heavily influenced by their expectations. Avoid the trap of looking for situations that will respond well to your favorite type of solution. Look objectively at the problems that confront you, try to understand them, and then determine what types of solutions would be appropriate. To evaluate all the aspects of your business, you can use Appendix C.

As a wise leader, you can see the real situation and circumstances with clarity. Be most sensitive to the important issues facing you and your company. Some may be internal and some external. Objectivity requires wisdom and honesty to understand what the key problems are. The concepts presented in this book can guide you in seeing your current situation from different perspectives.

Look closely at the developmental sequences shown in the road map to assess your current location or position, keeping in mind your product or service's market potential as your destination. This road map is designed to help you understand the management situation and how you might respond to it.

Just as an automobile's optimum speed depends on road conditions, your speed through these phases will be affected by various challenges you encounter in your management situation. Consider predictable problems as roadblocks or detours, and adjust your trip accordingly. The suggested phases of development are like recommended routes on freeways and highways. They are meant to be useful as a basic itinerary. But remember that your trip is unique.

Allow Objectives to Diverge

In the beginning, the business objectives of your organization are probably essentially the same as your own personal objectives. As you add more staff, the company grows and takes on a life of its own. Periodically review the original concepts of the business to see what your company's inception was based upon. It may have been to seek an opportunity in the marketplace, to be creative and aggressive, to validate your vision, or to change the world in some meaningful way.

As time goes by and your organization grows and matures, its objectives change. Factors that increase in importance are such essentials as financial solvency, customer and community relations, and supplier connections. These issues begin to overwhelm some of the earlier, perhaps more noble and exciting broad objectives. You may have to settle for high profitability rather than changing the world.

Another transition occurs when your leadership goals diverge from the goals of the organization. This divergence may be painful and difficult for both the leader and the company. Change is inevitable. Even if you decide not to grow but include a wider selection of other staff people, changes occur. The demographic forces of an organization will not allow it to stand still.

The first people you hire are more likely to be motivated by the challenge and excitement of being in a new venture. As you hire more people, your organization begins to reflect the general population from which you're drawing. As the staff population grows, people will become more interested in their own career development and salaries. While the fifth person you hire may be motivated by your vision, the fiftieth person will be motivated more by a desire to pay their mortgage.

Look for Deeper Issues

Look for the deeper truths that manifest themselves in daily problems. When you continue to have a certain type of problem, it may be an indicator of structural or cultural deficiencies. There is no naturally occurring force that will move you and your organization automatically from one mode of operation to the next. Instead, as your business moves through its various phases of development, you will see subtle clues that the need to change is building.

Certain types of problems, especially personnel problems, are sometimes an early indication of fundamental change. For example, problems concerning uncertainty about responsibility and authority could indicate that a Restructuring mode is needed.

Recurring issues about the lack of opportunity for individual qualified staff may indicate that your firm is too rigidly structured. Recurring problems about a lack of responsiveness to customers may mean that defiant isolation is a general weakness. Unmotivated staff may mean that the leadership allelopathy is not ebbing properly.

Some people in your organization might serve a function similar to canaries in a mine shaft. These are people who are highly sensitive to certain deficiencies or problems in an organization and who can provide warning signals indicating the issues you must deal with. Carefully consider any intensely delivered comments, especially if they are part of a developing trend. If you assume that all problems are only individual problems, you could miss early warning signs that bigger ones are looming on the horizon.

It is usually safe to assume that most people have good intentions and react with good reason to certain situations. Reviewing potential causes of structural and cultural problems will also help you check and recheck some of your basic assumptions about the decision-making environment or the developmental situation of your firm.

Use Business Momentum Wisely

Wise use of momentum is crucial because not all the phases of development generate business momentum. As discussed, Concept Development, Rapid Market Expansion, Market Stabilization, and Niche Development are momentum-building phases when the priority is to take advantage of market opportunities. The Foundation Building phase, however, has an internal focus and does not usually generate momentum.

Use the momentum generated during a momentum-building mode to carry you through each period of restructuring. When you restructure, you will need to turn away from market activities to focus on internal issues without jeopardizing your business. However, value what you do have and use those strengths because your competitor is going to be doing the same.

Some leaders who pride themselves on being business minded may view the internal orientation of the Foundation Building phase as less valuable and therefore may underemphasize it. Nonetheless, it is a crucial phase because it enables the culture and the structures of the organization to progress more effectively to the next momentum generating phase.

Anticipate Changes

Remember that the key role of the leader of a growing organization is to instigate appropriate changes before the need for those changes becomes imperative. Therefore, it is important to set different priorities for different times in advance. Anticipate changes in both your organization and its marketplace. Planning ahead is important because some of the changes needed to create each mode take time to develop.

Identify the right time to shake up the existing structure and culture of the organization and to introduce more appropriate attitudes, priorities, and capabilities. Initiate timely revolutions. Don't purge every aspect of the practices developed in the prior phases, but carry the benefits forward, and put down a new layer of capabilities when you move from phase to phase.

When you hire people, have an idea of how an individual's job and role will change over time. This will help both them and you to prepare for the requirements of those jobs. It also makes it less likely that some of these loyal individuals will become redundant as the organization evolves and so will also help to avoid the office manager crisis. Regulate the power of individuals to prevent a particular structure from becoming too embedded in the organization. Anticipate the broad changes that will need to take place to achieve your goals. Regulate the power of individuals to prevent a particular structure from becoming too embedded in the organization. Anticipate the broad changes that will need to take place to achieve your goals.

Once you've developed your broad base of capabilities by touching upon all the five different stages, you can go on to thrive in almost any kind of business environment you encounter.

Work Through Others

Work with and through others to help you meet the objectives of your organization. To change the structure, the decision-making roles, the way the work is divided up, or the nature of the work actually done, you must be able to work with and through other people. You will not be able to make all the changes alone.

Always discuss with your staff why a change is needed, what will be accomplished if the change is made, and what will be required to make the changes. Without this information, your shifts in priorities and modes of operation will confuse people. They need to understand what is taking place and why. Assure them that what took place in the past was not wrong but that it's just time for a different mode of operating. If you allow your staff to make conscious choices to be more successful and effective in the new situation, you'll be surprised how responsive your staff will be. They will know that you are not held captive by your character as a leader, and they won't be either.

When you create management teams, either formally or informally, you should try to both extend yourself and complement yourself. Identify people who share your energy, but also look for those who supplement your strengths with different ones of their own. Create teams that have various specific skills and perspectives, and set certain goals for them, clearly identifying what will be required for them to be successful.

Depend more on different people in different phases. You will need to develop specialized modes of operation during appropriate phases, so look for complementary skills and management style biases, and consider similar levels of energy and passions for success to give yourself more flexibility. Do not try to give all points of view equal weight at all times. To do so will not give you the competitive strength you will need at each phase. A team of diverse individuals will have a better chance of seeing what lies ahead and making the needed changes. It will help, however, to have everyone reading the same road map.

Sculpt the Culture of Your Organization

An organization's culture both reflects and affects the attitudes people have about how things should be done and which priorities to give a certain issue. When your staff members are deciding how to prioritize their work, make compromises, and interact with others, the organization's culture is often what tips the balance toward a certain direction.

The tribal instinct of humans is sometimes said to be the most powerful instinct we have. Creating and being part of a strong culture is part of belonging to a tribe. So be careful to design a positive tribal culture within your organization. Support people's decision-making efforts in a healthy way. Be flexible, but maintain a sense of community that helps guide people in their independent decision making.

Realize that, as a leader, you have a tremendous impact on the culture of the organization. Be very aware of the messages you send to others through your words and actions. Take an active interest in shaping the culture and mold one that supports long-term success. Understand that it is appropriate for you to be highly decisive at certain times and very slow and methodical at others. Ultimately, no single style of management should be so tightly woven into the culture of the organization that it cannot change. All must be represented.

Create an atmosphere of success. Reward people for responding to the true nature of problems. This will help the staff handle challenges with the idea that success and effectiveness are most important.

Broaden Your Range of Skills

Over the life of your business, you will need to operate in every mode of operation. You'll need to be able to set a variety of different priorities, some contrary to what you're personally most comfortable with or interested in. Consequently, you may need to broaden your range of leadership skills.

One of the best ways to do this is by emulating other people. You'll need to take cues from others and listen to what other people have to say. Identify people you can learn from and confer with them. Observe how they set priorities and operate in different modes.

Make sure you know yourself well. You can identify what your own biases are through the test in Appendix A. First find out which of the five modes you are naturally most comfortable with, then identify the mode that appears at the opposite corner of the diagram. This is your probable weak point, so you'll have to learn how to behave in that manner. For example, if you're highly conceptual and directive, try to develop analytic methods in your management. Take a chance. Be creative.

Talk to people who display that style, understand how they work, and observe their priorities. Then when the situation requires a style or an approach different from your usual one, you can call on the new skills you have developed in these experiences to tell you what direction is appropriate and help provide the needed kinds of leadership.

Make Natural Tendencies Pay

Given a freely moving labor market, people will gravitate to situations where they find comfort and success. The successive phases of business growth may require leaders to focus on issues that they probably don't enjoy or find interesting. People with any particular bias would find one or more of the phases quite boring or even intolerable.

Many entrepreneurs resist going through a new stage or making a change in their styles because they don't know if the change is going to be permanent or not. The fact that there are phases, however, presents the possibility that later phases may again be more personally gratifying. The key is to attend to the needs of the company, and then it can come back to a situation that's more comfortable and rewarding for the leader.

Just as you strive to create a situation that benefits from your personal preferences, also consider the interests of your staff. Find ways to make people's natural tendencies pay. While everyone can behave differently from their preferences when it is clearly to their advantage to do so, if you have them do what they enjoy, they will be more enthusiastic and productive. Use the tools in this book to understand your human resources and build on what you have or have access to.

Carl Survived the Journey

As Carl looks back now at all his company has gone through, all the different phases of growth, he is amazed. He never imagined when he began a few short years ago that he would have to go through so much to turn his flash of inspiration into a stable business. All he had wanted to do was to bring his idea into reality.

Now he sits in a finely appointed office and looks out onto a hive of activity in a state-of-the-art machine shop and busy assembly plant. Established products are being produced efficiently, new products are innovative, and the company is involved in relevant rapidly expanding markets.

"All of this started from just a single inspiration," he thought, but he also realized that the initial business has been transformed several times to get to where it is today. Those were challenging times. But with the help of his dedicated team, they were able to grow through these changes. "Whew," he thought. "I have survived."

Chapter 13

Going Beyond Success

Chapter 13

Going Beyond Success

It is important to define what success means to you. Success to one individual may be to have a thriving business, while success for another person may be to have a work environment that keeps them in their comfort zone. For some, it is to create a business environment that is custom-made to their own preferences; this is consistent with the common idea of being self-actualized by expressing one's own self and preferences in the day-to-day work environment. The entrepreneur who steers an organization through its various stages can't do this, however.

The successful entrepreneur who guides the company through the different growth phases described in this book must tolerate some discomfort. In fact, it may be a more personally pleasing path to be an unsuccessful or short-term leader of the organization. It may be easier and more comfortable to prevent the organization from growing to the point that a different style of leadership is required.

If you study management organizations, you see how the demographics of an organization change over time. People once thought they could identify their firm's most successful aspects and maintain their effectiveness and good performance by preserving these features — that is, by dipping their past successes in gold. However, the truth is that it's not possible to stay in one place. The market will change. Competitors will appear. The staff will gain experience and want to move into higher positions, forcing a change in the management of the company.

If the goal of entrepreneurs is to have economically successful organizations, there will be challenges to overcome. The willingness and ability to go beyond success in one phase distinguishes the successful entrepreneurs from the others. Exceptional leaders do what's best for their organization, even if the needed course of action is not consistent with their own preferences. These individuals are then not reacting to their own needs for self-expression but are responding to the true needs of the organization.

The information this book presents about the phases of business growth should help you avoid the roadblocks and take some of the error out of the trial-and-error that is sure to come as a result of your business successes.

Appendix A

Decision Style Inventory

Scoring Your Self Test

Interpreting Your Score

Appendix A

Decision Style Inventory

The focus of this exercise is to identify your preferred approach to making decisions. Of course, most people can and do make decisions in ways that are different from their most preferred approach. Nevertheless, it is important to know your preferences because you will often use your preferred approach in new or uncertain situations and when you believe you have a choice as to how a situation can be handled.

The following Decision Style Inventory was developed by Dr. Alan Rowe of the University of Southern California and is reprinted with his permission. Each question is answered by assigning the following points:

- 8 – most like you
- 4 – moderately like you
- 2 – little like you
- 1 – least like you

Each score can be assigned only once within each question, and all four numbers, 8, 4, 2 and 1, must be used for each question. For example, for the first question, you may assign the following scores:

My prime objective is to:

- Have a position with status   2
- Be the best in my field   1

Decision Style Inventory – Self Test*

	1		2		3		4
My prime objective is to:	Have a position with status.		Be the best in my field.		Achieve recognition for my work.		Feel secure in my job.
I enjoy jobs that:	Are technical and well-defined.		Have considerable variety.		Allow independent action.		Involve people.
I expect people working for me to be:	Productive and fast.		Highly capable.		Committed and responsive.		Receptive to suggestions.
In my job, I look for:	Practical results.		The best solutions.		New approaches and ideas.		Good working conditions.
I communicate best with others:	Orally and directly.		In writing.		By having a discussion.		In a group meeting.
In my planning I emphasize:	Current needs.		Meeting objectives.		Future goals.		Organizational needs.
When faced with solving a problem, I:	Rely on proven approaches.		Apply careful analysis.		Look for creative approaches.		Rely on my feelings.
When using information I prefer:	Specific facts.		Accurate and complete data.		Broad coverage of many opinions.		Limited data that is easily understood.
When I am uncertain about what to do, I:	Rely on hunch and intuition.		Search for facts.		Explore a possible compromise.		Delay making a decision.
Whenever possible, I avoid:	Long debates.		Incomplete work.		Using numbers or formulas.		Conflict with others.
I am especially good at:	Remembering dates and facts.		Solving difficult problems.		Seeing many possibilities.		Interacting with others.
When time is important, I:	Decide and act quickly.		Follow plans and priorities.		Refuse to be pressured.		Seek guidance or support.
In social settings, I:	Speak with others.		Think about what is being said.		Observe what is going on.		Listen to the conversation.
I am good at remembering:	People's names.		Places we met.		People's faces.		People's personalities.
The work I do provides me:	The power to influence others.		Challenging assignments.		Achieving my personal goal.		Acceptance by the group.
I work well with those who are:	Energetic and ambitious.		Punctual and confident.		Curious and open-minded.		Polite and trusting.
When under stress, I:	Become anxious.		Concentrate on the problem.		Become frustrated and annoyed.		Am concerned or forgetful.
Others consider me:	Aggressive and domineering.		Disciplined and precise.		Imaginative and perfectionist.		Supportive and compassionate.
My decisions are:	Realistic and impersonal.		Systematic and abstract.		Broad and flexible.		Sensitive to the needs of others.
I dislike:	Losing control.		Boring work.		Following rules.		Being rejected.
Totals	Column 1:		Column 2:		Column 3:		Column 4:

* Reprinted with permission from Dr. Alan Rowe.

- Achieve recognition for my work   4
- Feel secure in my job   8

There are no right or wrong answers. Each person is different and will, therefore, score the answers to each question differently. You should relax when filling out the inventory and recognize that it simply reflects your preferences. Generally, the first answer that comes to mind is the best one to put down.

Scoring Your Self Test

To score your responses, simply total the number in each of the four columns and enter the total in the boxes at the bottom of the questionnaire. The total for the first column is your score for the directive style. The second score is the analytic style. The third is the conceptual style, and the fourth the behavioral style. The combined scores should total 300 points.

Interpreting Your Score

Write your scores for each style on line A of the Decision Style Inventory Score Comparison chart, on the next page. On line B, put a #1 under the highest score and a #2 under the next highest. These are your dominant and backup styles, respectively, and are the styles you use most frequently. Place an X under the lowest score. This is your least preferred style, the style you use least often.

To determine how you compare to the average American, in each column circle the range of numbers in which the score falls in section C of the chart. The average scores for Americans are shown in section C, along with the percent of the population that has scores in the rage indicated.

Section D will help you determine if your combination of preferred decision styles is similar to the five different management styles defined in this book. Each row indicates the score typical of the management style indicated. Circle all that apply to you in the first column. Review each row to determine how closely you fit the five management styles discussed.

Your management style is one of the five styles listed if you are able to circle all the indicated ranges in each row for that management style. For example, if your directive score is 78, you fit within the range in the directive column for the decisive visionary but not the range indicated for the decisive commander. If you do not fit any of the five management styles defined, do not panic. Identify the management styles which are closest

Decision Style Inventory Score Comparison

	Directive	Analytical	Conceptual	Behavioral
A. Your Decision Style Score				
B. Relative Dominance				
C. Comparison to Average American				
Very high (15% of population)	90 and higher	105 and higher	95 and higher	70 and higher
High (15%)	82–89	97–104	87–94	62–69
Moderately high (20%)	75–81	90–96	80–86	55–61
Average	75	90	80	55
Moderately low (20%)	68–74	83–89	73–79	48–54
Low (15%)	60–67	75–82	65–72	40–47
Very low (15%)	59 and below	74 and below	64 and below	39 and below
D. Management Style				
Decisive visionary	75 and higher	Up to 90	87 and higher	
Collaborative engineer		90 and higher		55 and higher
Decisive commander	82 and higher			
Methodical engineer		97 and higher		
Collaborative visionary		83 and higher	87 and higher	55 and higher

to your preferred decision style combination; these will be the easiest for you to emulate.

Some people will be able to claim more than one management style. They can selectively emphasize different elements of their management style for different situations.

For a graphical representation of your scores, note the decision styles in section C for which you scored average or above, then on the Preferred Decision Styles Road Map, highlight or outline the ellipses on the diagram that correspond to your most naturally preferred styles. These ellipses circumscribe the management situations, phases of development, and modes of operation that you would find most comfortable and enjoyable as the leader of a venture. If the two marked ellipses cross each other, the area of crossover is an area of development in which you are probably most comfortable.

Next, note which styles scored low or very low in section C of the Decision Style Inventory Score Comparison and place an X over the

corresponding oval on the diagram. This corresponds to your least preferred territory, one in which you will need to be especially diligent and
determined in order to be effective. If none of your scores are high or
low relative to the average American, consider the dominance of styles
as indicted on line B of the scoring chart. This perspective considers
only your preference for one style over the preference for another.

Preferred Decision Styles Road Map

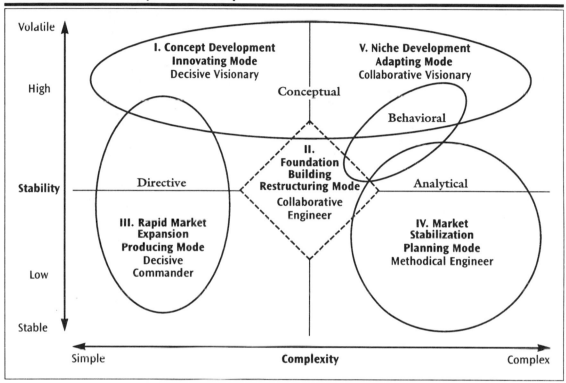

Appendix B

Assessing Business Culture and Structure

Assessing the Culture

Assessing the Structure

Assessing Business Culture and Structure

These two self tests will provide you with a quick way to identify your organization's cultural priorities and its structure.

Assessing the Culture

For each row in Assessing Cultural Priorities – Worksheet 1, allocate 20 points among the four statements A through D, according to how well each of the statements describes your current situation. Then total the numbers in each column to determine the dominance of each decision style as a description of your culture. For instance, this sample row of the worksheet describing your company's mission shows that 10 of the 20 points have been allocated to statement A, 0 points have been allocated to statement B, and 5 points each to statements C and D.

Assessing Cultural Priorities – Worksheet Sample

	A	B	C	D	Score
Mission.	Action, meeting specific and tangible objectives.	Thorough research, stability, seeking the right answer.	Flexility, ad-hoc efforts.	Getting everyone in-volved, agreement, good atmosphere.	
Scores:	10	0	5	5	20

Assessing Cultural Priorities – Worksheet 1

	A	B	C	D	Score
Typical motivation for dramatic new initiatives is:	You want that piece of business.	You can leverage your existing practices with little modification.	You can expand to new frontiers.	Your customers ask you to do it.	
Scores:					20
Acceptable sources of information for use in decisions are:	Existing facts.	Objective research data.	People's intuition.	Other people outside the organization.	
Scores:					20
Favored decision processes are:	Quick.	Well supported by objective facts.	Focused on new solutions.	Agreeable for all involved.	
Scores:					20
Acceptable justifications for business mistakes are:	What mistake? At least you could make a decision. You didn't waste a lot of time talking about what to do.	You implemented your disciplines. Your analysis drove your decisions. You did what you always do.	You tried something new. You were on the cutting edge.	All agreed to the course of action.	
Scores:					20
Valued behavior is:	Action, meeting specific and tangible objectives.	Thorough research, stability, seeking the right answer.	Flexibility, ad-hoc efforts.	Getting everyone involved, agreement, good atmosphere.	
Scores:					20
Totals:					100
Cultural bias in terms of management style and decision style	Decisive commander (directive style).	Methodical engineer (analytical style).	Creative visionary (conceptual style).	Collaborative facilitator (behavioral style).	

The highest scoring column indicates the management and decision styles that typify the formal and informal priorities of your organization. The next highest score represents the next influence, and so forth. For example, if column B has the most points, the methodical engineer management style and analytic decision style represent the majority of cultural priorities of your organization.

Assessing the Structure

Assessing Organizational Structure – Worksheet 2 can help you identify the current structure of your organization. Again, allocate 20 points for each row among the four statements A through D, according to how well each of the statements describes your current situation. Add the numbers in each column, then compare them to see which structures are dominant in your organization.

Assessing Organizational Structure – Worksheet 2

	A	B	C	D	Score
People are organized by:	A single, integrated effort.	Sales and non-sales activities.	Internal functions or products.	External market segments or some other feature outside the control of the organization.	
Scores:					20
Involvement in decision making.	Everyone votes, but only one vote counts.	Only one person decides and no voting takes place.	Key decisions are usually broken into smaller ones along the functional lines of a work process. Members make decisions about their functional areas. All their decisions are aggregated according to a comprehensive plan.	Key decisions are usually broken into smaller ones along segments of the external market, which are handled independently. Staff acts as semi-autonomous decision makers working across functions.	
Scores:					20
Most powerful people other than the leader are:	None, or the office manager.	Heads of the infrastructure departments, such as accounting, sales, production.	Heads of the major functional departments, such as manufacturing, design, marketing.	Staff in charge of the market segments, relationship managers, marketing staff, regional officers.	
Scores:					20
Rules that guide people in their decisions are:	Nonexistent.	Simple and very specific.	Policies, manuals, and plans that are the blue-prints for the way work should be done.	Clear, broad game rules that allow everyone to work together and define how success is measured. No centrally-defined implementation strategies.	
Scores:					20
Number of people reporting directly to leader.	Fewer than 10 people and that includes everyone involved in decision making.	Formally, about 10, but informally about twice that number.	5 to 10.	7 to 12.	
Scores:					20
Totals:					100
Organizational structure.	Team of focused generalists.	Platoon of implementors.	Hierarchy of functional groups.	Federation of market-driven teams.	

Creating Alignment

Transfer your answers from Assessing Cultural Priorities – Worksheet 1 and Assessing Organizational Structure – Worksheet 2 above and from the Preferred Decision Styles Road Map in Appendix A to the Current Status Assessment column below.

Current Status   **Assessment**

Your current culture:
Assessing Cultural Priorities – Worksheet 1 (Appendix B)   _____

Your current structure:
Assessing Organizational Structure – Worksheet 2 (Appendix B)   _____

Your current mode of operation:
Assessing Organizational Structure – Worksheet 2 (Appendix B)   _____

Your preferred decision style:
Decision Style Inventory Score Comparison (Appendix A)   _____

Now circle the phase of your business' development in the Ideal Alignment chart below. Read through the elements of each mode and compare them to what you wrote above to see if there are changes that you should consider making to bring your organization into alignment with the requirements of the situation.

Ideal Alignment

| phase: | I | II | III | IV | V |
mode:	Innovating	Restructuring	Producing	Planning	Adapting
Decision Style	Decisive visionary (conceptual with directive).	Collaborative engineer (analytic and behavioral).	Decisive commander (directive).	Methodical engineer (analytic).	Collaborative visionary (conceptual with behavioral).
Priority	Breakthrough Innovation.	Efficient and effective infrastructure.	Gaining market presence.	Well developed functional capabilities.	Responsive adaptation.
Structure	Tribe of generalists.	Functionally segmented team.	Platoon of implementors.	Pyramid of functional groups.	Federation of market-driven teams.
Important Control Mechanisms	Loyalty, vision, direct supervision.	Hierarchy, formal procedures.	Supervision, feedback and evaluation.	Explicit strategies hierarchy.	Vision, culture, feedback and evaluation.
Preconditions	Fewer than 10 people involved, little insulation from market environment.	Viable concept or product, sufficient business momentum.	Protection and stability.	Right rut, stability.	Inefficient information systems, customers willing to pay.

Appendix C

Evaluating Your Own Situation

The Path Thus Far

What Type of People Do You Have?

What Are Your Personal Objectives?

What Are Your Management Priorities?

What Are Your Firm's Cultural Priorities?

What Is Your Organization's Structure?

Is the Time Right for Restructuring?

Appendix C

Evaluating Your Own Situation

Selecting the right mode of operation and then creating it requires that you know where you are now and what you have to work with. To help you review your situation, this section will prompt your thinking about:

- Your organization's developmental path thus far,
- Types of people in your organization,
- The management and cultural priorities important in your organization, and
- Your organization's structure.

These topics, along with the list of undesirable legacies and the worksheets to assess your organization's culture and structure, will help you determine important issues to consider for change and development. With this information, you will gain a better sense of where you are on the road to entrepreneurial growth and which direction is best for you.

The Path Thus Far

To develop clarity and see your organization objectively, review the history of your firm's development and identify the legacies of the path that you have taken to get where you are now.

If your business is large or diverse, consider your most recently developed or most important business unit as opposed to trying to assess your entire business, which may be a mix of business initiatives at different developmental phases. Here is a summary of the phases to help you with your answer.

1. Concept Development. During the Innovating mode you serve pioneering customers with custom products. Your priority is a breakthrough innovation that addresses a significant unmet need in the marketplace.

2. Foundation Building. During the first Restructuring mode you serve pioneering customers. Your goals are to simplify your product, develop a business infrastructure, and select a pivotal market segment to target in the next phase.

3. Rapid Market Expansion. During the Producing mode you serve pragmatist customers with a single version of your innovation. Your priority is to gain market exposure faster than anyone else.

4. Market Stabilization. During the Planning mode you serve conservative customers with products that fit seamlessly in with their lives. Priorities are to refine production, lower costs, ensure consistency, and train staff.

5. Niche Development. During the Adapting mode you serve customers with diverse needs, the sophisticates. Priority is on developing customized solutions for profitable niches driven by market demand.

Is there a phase of business development that is clearly indicative of where your business is?

What type of dramatic changes have you recently seen in your organization's structure or your corporate culture?

How have you responded to new situations?

Was there a strong Concept Development phase of your organization when it was starting up and establishing a toehold in the market?

Did you go through a transitional restructuring period when you focused on internal issues?

During that transition, did you make sure that the basic business infrastructure was set in place and that it was efficient?

When did that restructuring happen?

How many people were employed in your organization during the first restructuring?

Has your organization successfully met the developmental objectives of each phase?

Did you cut one or two phases shorter than needed because they were uncomfortable or unfamiliar?

How far in the progression of phases has your main line of business come?

Did you skip any developmental phases?

Does your organization have well-developed innovative capabilities?

Is it an efficient producer of physical products?

Does it provide excellent customer service?

Are there any latent structural deficiencies in your organization that prevent it from taking advantage of future business opportunities?

What Type of People Do You Have?

Remember that the business environment is dynamic and your organization changes simply because of the passage of time. People get older and usually gain higher levels of expertise. These changes cause your firm to evolve because what you have to work with has changed. In addition, your staff's personal career objectives change.

Look at the people you have in your organization and answer these questions.

Have you gathered a large number of people who simply do your bidding, or are they truly independent decision makers?

Are your employees creative and always looking for a new solution?

Do employees tend to do a lot of thorough research before making decisions, or do they make decisions then gather research to support their decision?

Do you have only certain types of people working in certain areas of the company?

Do you have people of a similar age, decision style, or level of expertise?

Do you find that the people you hired in certain stages have now progressed and moved on to other kinds of functions for which they are not particularly qualified?

What are the methods that your organization emphasizes to control the activities of staff?

Does your organization favor the highly articulate individuals who can give well researched and thoughtful answers?

Does your organization tolerate the idiosyncratic and seemingly scattered innovative types?

Do you place a high value on personnel issues and training?

What Are Your Personal Objectives?

To look at your own objectives and determine where you would like to go as a leader, consider these questions.

Are your personal objectives and your objectives for the company similar?

Are your objectives and your company's objectives compatible?

If there is close alignment between your personal objectives and the company's objectives, how much are others able to participate in your objectives?

Do you make it possible for others to expand their own horizons, take part in leadership, and feel a greater sense of fulfillment and commitment, or are you setting up the organization primarily to meet your own objectives?

What kind of people should you be hiring in order to meet those differing objectives

Are you building an organization that will live beyond your current needs and objectives?

What Are Your Management Priorities?

To assess the management priorities within your organization, start with the three most recent major problems that your organization has addressed and think about how your organization went about solving them. Consider typical priorities of each decision style and choose which of the following approaches best describes how you handled each of your three most recent major problems.

- You acted by taking the first step that seemed as though it would solve the problem. This is a decisive commander management style and a directive decision style.
- You performed careful analysis to understand the key components of the problem and to identify in a logical way what should be done. This is a methodical engineer management style and an analytic decision style.
- You took an innovative approach, seeking to come up with a new answer. This would indicate a creative visionary management style and a conceptual decision style.
- You reviewed the opinions of internal or external experts. This is a collaborative facilitator management style and a behavioral decision style.

Looking back at those three problems, did they actually require the kind of solution or attention that they ultimately received?

If they didn't, was the solution driven by personal preference?

If all three problems received the same kind of solution, was it because there is a lack of variety in your responses or that singular priorities exist in your organization?

Would other approaches to leadership have been more effective?

Now, considering your organizations three biggest successes, are there trends in what you did?

Regarding how your firm manages both a new product and an old product, is your firm handling the two in the same manner, with the same decision structure and cultural emphasis?

Did you let each situation drive its solution, or did your organization superimpose a solution on them?

How much decision-making flexibility does your organization have?

Does your organization value different approaches to management?

How much emphasis does your organization place on displaying a certain kind of management style?

What Are Your Firm's Cultural Priorities?

Your organization's cultural priorities reflect the memory of what has been successful and what has not. They are forces that influence how people act and indicate what is or is not acceptable behavior based on what has been successful in the past.

What are the key priorities embedded in the culture?

Is it a priority to be defiantly innovative, ignoring current practices and market wisdom or to be highly sensitive to market conditions, opportunities, and other external forces?

Is the priority simply to gain market share and press your product into the marketplace, or is it to be deliberate, organized, and thorough about making decisions?

How does the culture of the organization compare to your style of management?

What are the strongest similarities and the most prominent differences?

Can the culture of your organization adapt to the changes of the environment, regardless of your personal priorities?

Does your organization have biases similar to your own?

Does it place high priority on the same issues as you do?

Another way to assess the firm's organizational culture is to have everyone complete the decision style questionnaire included in this book, and then look at the average scores of the people who have been there the longest or who are the cultural leaders of the firm. This will give you a good idea of the priorities that are being set and reinforced on a day-to-day basis.

What Is Your Organization's Structure?

To review your decision-making structures, think about how you organize your work and your people, then ask yourself these questions.

Are people organized by functions or are they organized in customer-oriented teams?

After you've introduced multiple products, have you developed a functional organization where a particular functional group serves a variety of products?

What control mechanisms are most important in your organization?

Is the structure of your organization consistent with the kind of structure that you personally prefer?

If you thrive on rigid structure, is your organization too rigid to meet the demands of the current situation?

If you have a large, diverse organization, are there blind spots built into your organization?

If you tend to avoid highly structured situations, is your firm avoiding needed structure?

Is the Time Right for Restructuring?

Assess the trajectory and momentum of your business to see if you might sustain a period of restructuring.

Trajectory

If your business has positive trajectory, you may have opportunities to make changes or address needs that may have gone unmet during earlier periods. If you have a negative trajectory, you may simply need to focus on addressing recent performance problems.

Have you had recent business successes?

Has your business been particularly effective during a recent period?

Momentum

Use periods of high momentum to prepare for future needs. Don't wait for your business momentum to run out before making the needed changes.

Have you developed good will among your clients and customers?

Do you have a strong position in the market that will allow you to sustain a Restructuring phase when you can shift some of your management attention to internal issues?

Index

ESTABLISH A FRAMEWORK
FOR EXCELLENCE
WITH THE OASIS PRESS ®

OASIS PRESS
BOOKS & SOFTWARE
Celebrating 25 Years

THE OASIS PRESS'
PSI RESEARCH
P.O. BOX 3727
CENTRAL POINT, OR
97502-0032

Fastbreaking changes in technology and the global marketplace continue to create unprecedented opportunities for businesses through the '90s and into the new millennium. However with these opportunities will also come many new challenges. Today, more than ever, businesses, especially small businesses, need to excel in all areas of operation to complete and succeed in an ever-changing world.

The Successful Business Library takes you through the '90s and beyond, helping you solve the day-to-day problems you face now, and prepares you for the unexpected problems you may be facing down the road. With any of our products, you will receive up-to-date and practical business solutions, which are easy to use and easy to understand. No jargon or theories, just solid, nuts-and-bolts information.

Whether you are an entrepreneur going into business for the first time or an experienced consultant trying to keep up with the latest rules and regulations, The Successful Business Library provides you with the step-by-step guidance, and action-oriented plans you need to succeed in today's world. As an added benefit, PSI Research/The Oasis Press® unconditionally guarantees your satisfaction with the purchase of any book or software application in our catalog.

More than a marketplace for our products, we actually provide something that many business Web sites tend to overlook... useful information!

It's no mystery that the World Wide Web is a great way for businesses to promote their products, however most commercial sites stop there. We have always viewed our site's goals a little differently. For starters, we have applied our 25 years of experience providing hands-on information to small businesses directly to our Web site. We offer current information to help you start your own business, guidelines to keep it up and running, useful federal and state-specific information (including addresses and phone numbers to contact these resources), and a forum for business owners to communicate and network with others on the Internet. We would like to invite you to check out our Web site and discover the information that can assist you and your small business venture.

The Oasis Press Online
http://www.psi-research.com

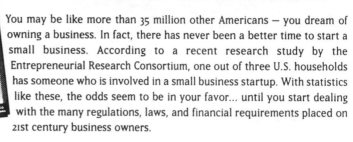

From The Leading Publisher of Small Business Information
Books that save you time and money.

Managers and business owners will learn exactly where to draw the line on sexual harassment. How to draw the line firmly, so that employees understand and respect it. Clearly spells out the procedures that are most effective if a lawsuit is lodged and gives tips on enlisting a good attorney.

Draw The Line   **Pages: 172**
Paperback: $17.95   **ISBN: 1-55571-370-X**

This useful guide discusses techniques for developing a solid foundation on which to build a successful business. Includes many real-world pointers that any business can implement into its day-to-day operations. Contains 30 checklists, evaluations, figures, and charts that will give you the power to drive your business' profits in the right direction.

Profit Power   **Pages: 272**
Paperback: $19.95   **ISBN: 1-55571-374-2**

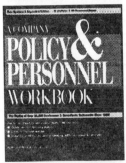

Saves costly consultant or staff hours in creating company personnel policies. Provides over 70 model policies on topics such as employee safety, leave of absence, flex time, smoking, substance abuse, sexual harassment, performance improvement, and grievance procedures. For each subject, practical and legal ramifications are explained and a choice of alternate policies is presented.

Company Policy & Personnel Workbook   **Pages: 350**
Paperback: $29.95   **ISBN: 1-55571-365-3**
Binder: $49.95   **ISBN: 1-55571-364-5**

This authoritative guide will transform the roles of administrators and improve effectiveness for corporate, nonprofit, and community organizations, many of which are over-managed but lack effective leadership. Its skills-oriented solutions teach managers to be effective leaders and train leaders to be better managers — a distinction often overlooked by other management guides.

The Leader's Guide: 15 Essential Skills   **Pages: 250**
Paperback: $19.95   **ISBN: 1-55571-434-X**

ALL MAJOR CREDIT CARDS ACCEPTED

CALL TO PLACE AN ORDER
— or —
TO RECEIVE A FREE CATALOG   **1-800-228-2275**

International Orders (541) 479-9464   *Fax Orders* (541) 476-1479
Web site http://www.psi-research.com   *Email* sales@psi-research.com

PSI Research   P.O. Box 3727   Central Point, Oregon   97502   U.S.A.

From The Leading Publisher of Small Business Information
Books that save you time and money.

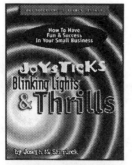